HANGED AT LEEDS

STEVE FIELDING

The History Press

First published 2009

The History Press
The Mill, Brimscombe Port
Stroud, Gloucestershire, GL5 2QG
www.thehistorypress.co.uk

© Steve Fielding, 2009

The right of Steve Fielding to be identified as the Author of this work
has been asserted in accordance with the Copyrights, Designs and
Patents Act 1988.

All rights reserved. No part of this book may be reprinted or reproduced
or utilised in any form or by any electronic, mechanical or other
means, now known or hereafter invented, including photocopying and
recording, or in any information storage or retrieval system, without the
permission in writing from the Publishers.

British Library Cataloguing in Publication Data.
A catalogue record for this book is available from the British Library.

ISBN 978 0 7509 5093 0

Typesetting and origination by The History Press
Printed in Great Britain

CONTENTS

About the Author   7

Acknowledgements   8

Research Material & Sources   9

Introduction   11

1. Behind Closed Doors   17
   William Smedley, 21 December 1875
2. Hanged Twice   18
   John Henry Johnson, 3 April 1877
3. 'For That I Done But Never Intended'   20
   Charles Frederick Peace, 25 February 1879
4. Drunken Passion   23
   James Hall, 23 May 1881
5. Cruelty at Sea   24
   Osmond Otto Brand, 23 May 1882
6. 'All Through Drink'   25
   Joseph Laycock, 26 August 1884
7. 'A Bonny Mess in that House!'   27
   Henry Hobson, 22 August 1887
8. The Unlucky One   28
   James William Richardson, 22 May 1888
9. 'I Done for Her, I'll Swing for Her'   29
   Charles Bulmer, 1 January 1889
10. 'Acting at Jack the Ripper!'   30
    Frederick Brett, 31 December 1889
11. 'Blame Yourself and Leicester Jack'   31
    Robert West, 31 December 1889
12. On Account of the Provocation   32
    James Harrison, 26 August 1890
13. A Mother's Duty   33
    Walter Lewis Turner, 18 August 1891
14. The Linthwaite Murder   35
    James Stockwell, 5 January 1892
15. 'Now No One Else Can Have Her'   36
    Henry Pickering, 14 June 1892
16. On a Lonely Road   37
    Moses Cudworth, 18 August 1892
17. On Her Birthday   38
    Edward Hemmings, 4 April 1893
18. For That Purpose   39
    Phillip Garner, 3 April 1894

19.	'For a Deed I Never Done' *Alfred Dews, 21 August 1894*	40
20.	'Even if I Have to Lose my Life for it' *Patrick Morley, 31 December 1895*	41
21.	Like an Infuriated Animal *Joseph Robert Ellis, 25 August 1896*	42
22.	'A Gun and Six Penneth of Laudanum' *Joseph Robinson, 17 August 1897*	43
23.	A Gesture of Goodwill *Walter Robinson, 17 August 1897*	43
24.	'Big Enough to Hold Them and Me and All' *Thomas Mellor, 16 August 1900*	44
25.	The First Bullet *Charles Benjamin Backhouse, 16 August 1900*	45
26.	The Beeston Tragedy *Charles Oliver Blewitt, 28 August 1900*	47
27.	'The Natural Avenger and Protector' *John Gallagher & Emily Swann, 29 December 1903*	48
28.	A Trail of Blood *James Henry Clarkson, 29 March 1904*	50
29.	Her Other Men *John Thomas Kay, 16 August 1904*	51
30.	The Son-in-Law *Edmund Hall, 20 December 1904*	52
31.	The Poachers *Arthur Jeffries, 28 December 1904*	53
32.	'If you Scream, I Will Kill you' *Thomas George Tattersall, 15 August 1905*	54
33.	The Ilkley Murder *George Smith, 28 December 1905*	55
34.	'Just a Bit of Bother' *John William Ellwood, 3 December 1908*	57
35.	'As Dead as a Mackerel' *Thomas Mead, 12 March 1909*	58
36.	'For This Piece of Paper' *John Raper Coulson, 9 August 1910*	59
37.	All Over a Sovereign *Henry Ison, 29 December 1910*	60
38.	Murder on the Farm *John William Thompson, 27 March 1917*	61
39.	Jealousy *Robert Gadsby, 18 April 1917*	63
40.	In a Drunken Rage *John William Walsh, 17 December 1918*	64
41.	An Unfaithful Wife *Benjamin Hindle Benson, 7 January 1919*	66
42.	The Deserters *Percy George Barrett & George William Cardwell, 8 January 1919*	67

43. With Great Provocation?   69
   Louis Massey, 6 January 1920
44. Underneath the Arches   70
   Miles McHugh, 16 April 1920
45. Plans for a New Life   71
   Thomas Hargreaves Wilson, 6 May 1920
46. Murder on the Dancefloor   72
   Edwin Sowerby, 30 December 1920
47. Murder at the Chinese Laundry   74
   Lee Doon, 5 January 1923
48. 'I Believe it is Murder'   75
   John William Eastwood, 28 December 1923
49. The Gigolo   76
   William Horsley Wardell, 18 June 1924
50. 'A Lot of Bother with a Woman'   78
   Alfred Davis Bostock, 3 September 1925
51. The Sheffield Hooligans   79
   Wilfred Fowler, 3 September 1925, & Lawrence Fowler, 4 September 1925
52. Yet Another Disagreement   82
   Lorraine Lax, 7 January 1926
53. A Fatal Bullet   83
   William Cornelius Jones, 5 January 1927
54. The End of an Affair   84
   Arthur Harnett, 2 September 1927
55. A Friend of the Family   85
   Samuel Case, 7 January 1928
56. Absent Without Leave   87
   Arthur Leslie Raveney, 14 August 1929
57. The Moneylender   89
   Frederick Gill, 4 February 1931
58. 'We Had a Quarrel…'   91
   Thomas Riley, 28 April 1932
59. At the Piggeries   92
   John Henry Roberts, 28 April 1932
60. A Reign of Terror   94
   Ernest Brown, 6 February 1934
61. The Boxing Day Murder   97
   Lewis Hamilton, 6 April 1934
62. Put Away Quietly   98
   Frederick Rushworth, 1 January 1935
63. A Terrible Secret   100
   David Maskill Blake, 7 February 1935
64. His Girl   102
   Andrew Anderson Bagley, 10 February 1937
65. Death at the Fairground   104
   Trevor Elvin, 10 September 1943
66. The Vital Clue   105
   Mervin Clare McEwen, 3 February 1944

67. The Killer with Blood Group 'A' — 107
   Arthur Thompson, 31 January 1945
68. Through Jealousy — 109
   Thomas Eric Richardson, 7 September 1945
69. Home from the War — 110
   William Batty, 8 January 1946
70. The Most Sordid of Motives — 113
   Albert Sabin, 30 January 1947
71. Witness for the Prosecution — 115
   Eric Charles Briggs, 20 June 1947
72. Two Motives — 117
   William Smedley, 14 August 1947
73. A 'Spiv and a Wide-Boy' — 118
   John Edward Gartside, 21 August 1947
74. Some form of Insanity — 120
   George Henry Whelpton, 7 January 1948
75. Hanged on His Birthday — 123
   Arthur George Osborne, 30 December 1948
76. The Boyfriend — 127
   Dennis Neville, 2 June 1949
77. Gangsters — 129
   Walter Sharpe, 30 March 1950
78. To Catch a Thief — 131
   Alfred Moore, 6 February 1952
79. In the Nick of Time — 133
   Philip Henry, 30 July 1953
80. Payback — 135
   Robert William Moore, 5 January 1954
81. 'I Lost my Control' — 137
   Wilhelm Lubina, 27 January 1954
82. Suspect Number One — 138
   Albert George Hall, 22 April 1954
83. The Lodgers — 141
   Edward Lindsay Reid, 1 September 1954
84. The Safe House — 142
   Winston Shaw, 4 May 1955
85. The Mother-in-Law — 143
   Alec Wilkinson, 12 August 1955
86. Overwhelming Evidence — 146
   Ernest Raymond Jones, 10 February 1959
87. Singled Out by Fate — 148
   Bernard Hugh Walden, 14 August 1959
88. A Win on the Pools — 150
   Zsiga Pankotai, 29 June 1961

   Appendix I: Public Executions at Leeds Armley Gaol 1864–1868 — 154

   Appendix II: Private Executions at Leeds Armley Gaol 1875–1961 — 156

   Index — 159

ABOUT THE AUTHOR

Steve Fielding was born in Bolton, Lancashire in the 1960s. He attended Bolton County Grammar School and served an apprenticeship as an engineer before embarking on a career as a professional musician. After many years of recording and touring, both in Great Britain and Europe, most notably with punk rock band The Stiffs, he began writing in 1993 and had his first book published a year later. He is the author of eighteen books on the subject of true crime, and in particular hangmen and executions.

He compiled the first complete study of modern-day executions, *The Hangman's Record 1868–1964* (Chancery House Press, 1994) and, as well as writing a number of regional murder casebooks, he is also the author of two books on executioners: *Pierrepoint: A Family of Executioners* (Blake, 2006) and *The Executioner's Bible: Hangmen of the 20th Century* (Blake, 2007). He has worked as a regular contributor to magazines such as the *Criminologist*, *Master Detective* and *True Crime* and as the Historical Consultant on the Discovery Channel series *The Executioners*, and *Executioner: Pierrepoint* for the Crime & Investigation channel. He has also appeared on *Dead Strange* (Southern Television) and BBC1's *The One Show*. Besides writing he also teaches at a local college.

Hanged at Leeds is the fifth in a series and follows *Hanged at Durham*, *Hanged at Pentonville*, *Hanged at Liverpool* and *Hanged at Manchester*.

Previous titles in the series:

Forthcoming titles in the series include:

> Hanged at Birmingham
> Hanged at Wandsworth
> Hanged at Winchester

ACKNOWLEDGEMENTS

I would like to thank the following people for help with this book. Firstly to Lisa Moore for her help in every stage in the production, but mainly with the photographs and proofreading. I offer my sincere thanks again to both Tim Leech and Matthew Spicer, who have been willing to share information along with rare documents, photographs and illustrations from their own collections. I would also like to acknowledge the help given by Janet Buckingham, who helped to input the original data.

RESEARCH MATERIAL & SOURCES

As with my other books on capital punishment and executions, many people have supplied information and photographs over the years, some of whom have since passed away. I remain indebted to the help with rare photographs and material given to me by the late Syd Dernley (assistant executioner), and former prison officer the late Frank McKue.

The bulk of the research for this book was done many years ago and extra information has been added to my database as and when it has become available. In most instances contemporary local and national newspapers have supplied the basic information, which has been supplemented by material found in PCOM, HO and ASSI files held at the National Record Office at Kew. I have been fortunate to have access to the Home Office Capital Case File 1901–1948, along with personal information in the author's collection from those directly involved in some of the cases.

Space doesn't permit a full bibliography of books and websites accessed whilst researching this project. I have tried to locate the copyright owners of all images used in this book, but a number of them were untraceable. In particular, I have been unable to locate the copyright holders of a number of images sourced from the National Archives. I apologise if I have inadvertently infringed any existing copyright.

INTRODUCTION

HMP Leeds, located in the Armley district, two miles from the city centre, became a place of execution when the city began to host Assize Courts in 1864. Built from locally quarried stone, the prison was designed by architects Messrs Perkin and Backhouse of Leeds and completed in July 1847. The castellated twin tower gate was said to give the prison the air of a medieval fortress and it was originally densely surrounded by rows of grim terraced housing, mostly now long since demolished. In 1901, a newspaper reported the prison's appearance as 'grim but grand' and likened it architecturally to Windsor Castle.

Housing four wings (A–D) radiating from a central point in a 'panoptical design', typical of the prisons built in that era, it allowed a gaoler to stand in the centre area and have a clear view down each wing. The wings had three landings and contained a total of 334 cells, one for each inmate. More cells were added over the years as the size of the gaol increased to cope with demand.

Armley Gaol originally housed both men and women prisoners and a report in 1869 noted that, 'in recent times the female prisoners have been more unruly than the males, and much more difficult to control.' Those termed 'Refractory Females' were punished in the stocks. The gaol also held inmates of both sexes as young as 12 years old. Inmates took part in a variety of tasks; those with trades or proven skills were put to task in the workshops, while prisoners with no regular occupation were employed picking oakum or making matting.

The one and only public execution at the gaol took place in 1864 (*see* Appendix I) and by 1875 executions began to take place in private at the gaol. Prior to this, those convicted at Leeds had mostly been transferred to York for execution.

*

The first hangman to officiate at Leeds was local man Thomas Askern, who had been carrying out public executions around the region for many years. Askern had satisfactorily carried out the public double execution in 1864 and also that of William Smedley in 1875 at Leeds, when he was engaged to hang John Johnson in April 1877. Askern botched the execution badly (*see* Chapter 2) and was sacked, to be replaced at the prison for the next execution by William Marwood; acknowledged as the pioneer of the 'long drop' method of execution, which caused instant death by a broken neck rather than painful strangulation his predecessors had preferred with a shorter rope and therefore shorter drop.

Marwood officiated at the just three executions at the gaol and, following his death in 1883, applications were invited for a man to replace him as the Hangman of England. The man chosen was Bartholomew Binns of Dewsbury, whose brief reign lasted less than a year. During the time, Binns travelled the country botching executions on a regular basis until he was dismissed following a drunken escapade at Liverpool and replaced by another Yorkshireman, James Berry of Bradford. However, in August 1884, when Leeds had a man under sentence of death, Berry was unable to officiate due to

Armley Gaol in Victorian times. (T.J. Leech Archive)

a prior engagement and the position was given to James Billington of Bolton, Lancashire, who had failed in his application to replace Marwood a year before, but who had applied to prison governors asking to be given a chance should they need an executioner. Billington carried out the execution to everyone's satisfaction and he was called to officiate at all subsequent executions into the twentieth century, despite the country's chief executioner living just a few miles from the gaol. It was a trend that Leeds would adopt throughout the next century: Billington was the executioner at Leeds while James Berry worked as the chief executioner across the country; Tom Pierrepoint was second to John Ellis as the country's chief executioner and while Albert Pierrepoint officiated at most prisons after the war, Leeds preferred to use the inexperienced Steve Wade.

James Billington died in 1901 and was succeeded as chief executioner by his sons, William and John. In 1905, John Billington suffered a tragic accident while on duty at the gaol, which was to cost him his life (*see* Chapter 32). The Billington dynasty was then replaced by that of the Pierrepoints. Henry Pierrepoint, who was living in Bradford at the time, initially replaced John Billington, and when he himself was dismissed in 1910 following a brawl at an execution in Essex, he was in due turn replaced by his brother, Thomas, who was to become the longest-serving hangman of the twentieth century and who carried out more executions than any other man at the gaol: thirty-two, including three doubles.

Tom Pierrepoint was then succeeded by Steve Wade of Doncaster. Wade was pensioned off in 1955 to be replaced by Harry Allen for the final three executions. Interestingly, although often credited as being so, neither Henry nor Tom Pierrepoint were Yorkshiremen, having been born in Nottingham, likewise neither was Steve Wade, who was born across the border in Manchester. The only modern-day Yorkshire-born hangmen to officiate at the gaol were Albert Pierrepoint, born in Bradford in 1905, and who made one brief appearance at the gaol in 1953, when Wade was unable to officiate through illness, and Harry Allen, who was born to Scottish parents at Denby Dale, West Yorkshire, and who spent his early childhood in the county before returning to Scotland and then crossing the border to spend his adult life in Lancashire.

A number of Yorkshiremen did work as assistants at the gaol. In 1892, Thomas Henry Scott, a rope maker from Mold Green, Huddersfield, assisted at the execution of Moses Cudworth. Having assisted Berry at a number of executions, Scott worked mainly in Ireland as a chief executioner, but following a tightening up by the Home Office at the turn of the century, all executioners had to apply for training if they wished to continue to work. Scott had been reported by more than one prison governor as having a drink problem and was not invited to apply.

INTRODUCTION

```
Memorandum of Conditions to which any Person acting as
Assistant Executioner is required to conform
```

(An Assistant Executioner will not be employed by the Governor without the concurrence of the High Sheriff)

1. An Assistant Executioner is engaged, with the concurrence of the High Sheriff, by the Governor of the prison at which the execution is to take place, and is required to conform with any instructions he may receive from or on behalf of the High Sheriff in connection with any execution for which he may be engaged.

2. A list of persons competent for the office of Assistant Executioner is in the possession of High Sheriffs and Governors: it is therefore unnecessary for any person to make application for employment in connection with an execution, and such application will be regarded as objectionable conduct and may lead to the removal of the applicant's name from the list.

3. Any person engaged as an Assistnat Executioner will report himself at the prison at which an execution for which he has been engaged is to take place not later than 4 o'clock on the afternoon preceding the day of execution.

4. He is required to remain in the prison from the time of his arrival until the completion of the execution and until permission is given him to leave.

5. During the time he remains in the prison he will be provided with lodging and maintenance on an approved scale.

6. He should avoid attracting public attention in going to or from the prison; he should clearly understand that his conduct and general behaviour must be respectable and discreet, not only at the place and time of execution, but before and subsequently. In particular he must not reveal to any person, whether for publication or not, any information about his work as an Assistant Executioner or any information which may come his way in the course of his duty. If he does he will render himself liable to prosecution under the Official Secrets Acts, 1911 and 1920.

7. His remuneration will be £2 12s. 6d. for the performance of the duty required of him, to which will be added £2 12s. 6d. if his conduct and behaviour have been satisfactory. The latter part of the fee will not be payable until a fortnight after the execution has taken place.

8. Record will be kept of his conduct and efficiency on each occasion of his being employed, and this record will be at the disposal of any Governor who may have to engage an assistant executioner.

9. The name of any person who does not give satisfaction, or whose conduct is in any way objectionable, so as to cast discredit on himself, either in connection with the duties or otherwise, will be removed from the list.

10. The apparatus approved for use at executions will be provided at the prison. No part of it may be removed from the prison, and no apparatus other than approved apparatus must be used in connection with any execution.

11. The Assistant Executioner will give such information, or make such record of the occurrences as the Governor of the prison may require.

Terms and conditions an assistant executioner must adhere to. This copy was signed by Doncaster hangman Harry Smith. (T.J. Leech Archive)

In 1911 Albert Lumb of Bradford applied to join the list of hangmen and was a regular assistant to both Tom Pierrepoint and John Ellis until the outbreak of the First World War, when his name disappeared from the short list of qualified hangmen. It would be 1950 before another Yorkshireman joined the list, when Harry Smith, a neighbour and presumably friend of Steve Wade passed out from the hangman's training school at London's Pentonville Prison. Smith assisted at many executions at Leeds and also assisted at the execution of Yorkshire-born mass murderer John Reginald Christie, who was hanged at Pentonville in 1953. Joseph Broadbent of Bradford became an assistant hangman in the summer of 1953, but his reign only lasted a little over a year. He assisted at the last double execution in England, at Pentonville in 1954, but when he was contacted with the offer to hang Alec

Assistant hangman Harry Smith assisted at the majority of post-war executions at the prison. (Author's collection)

weight of the prisoners with clothes.	Executioners length of drop.	weight of Prisoners with clothes	Executioners length of drop	weight of Prisoners with clothes.	Executioners length of drop.
lbs.	ft ins	lbs	ft ins	lbs	ft ins
118 + under	8 6	143	7 0	182	5 6
119 "	8 5	145	6 11	185	5 5
120 "	8 4	146	6 10	188	5 4
121 "	8 3	148	6 9	190	5 3
122 "	8 2	150	6 8	194	5 2
124 "	8 1	152	6 7	197	5 1
125 "	8 0	154	6 6	200	5 0
126 "	7 11	156	6 5		
128 "	7 10	158	6 4		
129 "	7 9	160	6 3		
130 "	7 8	162	6 2		
132 "	7 7	164	6 1		
133 "	7 6	167	6 0		
135 "	7 5	169	5 11		
136 "	7 4	171	5 10		
138 "	7 3	174	5 9		
140 "	7 2	176	5 8		
141 "	7 1	179	5 7		

A hangman's personal table of drops, dating from the 1940s. (Author's collection)

INTRODUCTION

The scaffold at Leeds in the Victorian era would have been the same as this gallows from Newgate. (Prison Service Museum)

Wilkinson at Leeds in 1955, Broadbent wrote that he did not wish to accept the engagement and that he would be sending in his resignation to the Prison Commissioners. Harry Smith offered his resignation in 1959, shortly after he assisted at the execution of Ernest Jones at Leeds.

*

Apart from the botched execution of John Johnson, there were other incidents on the gallows at the prison. In 1931, Frederick Gill put up such a struggle on the way to the gallows that the newspaper reported it took officials fifteen minutes to get the prisoner from the condemned cell to the drop. Gill was hanged in the execution shed adjacent to A Wing, which had been first used at the execution of Walter Turner in 1891. Leaving the condemned cell, the prisoner had to walk across the prison yard to the gallows, a distance of some 40 yards. Although this had been commonplace in Victorian times, by the 1940s it was one of the few prisons where the condemned man faced such a long walk to his death. Prior to this, the scaffold used in the first executions was erected in the grounds close to the prison hospital on D Wing, which also held the condemned cells.

For a time before the First World War Wakefield took over as the main centre of execution for Yorkshire and few hangings took place at Leeds. Wakefield's status was reclassified during the war and Leeds took over as the sole hanging gaol for this part of the region.

In 1949, while Wade was preparing the gallows for the execution of Dennis Neville, the rope broke during the test drop and another was hastily acquired to allow the execution to go ahead as planned on the following morning.

The last execution in this shed took place in March 1950, when Walter Sharpe was hanged for the murder of a jeweller in the previous year. For the next eighteen months anyone convicted at Leeds was sent to Manchester for execution while a new purpose-built execution suite was constructed in the prison grounds. The block was separate from the main prison building, which allowed the prison to execute away from other inmates, and it also housed the executioner's quarters. The first person executed on the new gallows was Alfred Moore. During the Winter Assizes of 1953, the newly built execution block found it could not cope with demand as four men were convicted at the same assizes. Two were sent to Manchester for execution, the other two were hanged at Leeds.

An LPC4 sheet was used to record every execution at the gaol. This records that of Bernard Walden in 1959 and notes that the assistant failed in his duties. (Author's collection)

Following the abolition of the death penalty in the 1960s, the block was re-commissioned as an administrative centre and also houses the prison dog unit, who, so I am told, also exercise in the area at the far end of the gaol where the condemned prisoners are buried.

*

By the mid-1970s the gaol was reported as being too small for the demands made on it and its function became mainly one of a short stay prison, where inmates were processed, catergorised and moved on to other prisons to complete their sentence. Movements at the gaol were so commonplace that it became known as 'the great transit camp', and one newspaper labeled it 'the Clapham Junction of the North!'.

In 1990, the Howard League for Penal Reform announced that it would conduct its own independent inquiry into the deaths of five teenage prisoners at the gaol following a refusal by the Home Office to hold a public inquiry. In April 2004, Shahid Aziz was murdered by his racist cell-mate at HMP Leeds. They had been sharing a cell for less than an hour when the attack took place. The killer was later sentenced to life imprisonment and moved to a different gaol.

HMP Leeds serves magistrates and Crown Courts in West Yorkshire, parts of North Yorkshire and South Yorkshire, and takes prisoners from across the Pennines in Lancashire and Greater Manchester. Recent expansion has seen the prison increase in size, taking the number of inmates to over 1,200 and making it one of the largest prisons in the country.

This book looks at the cases of ninety men and one woman who, following the Private Executions Act of 1868, were all *Hanged at Leeds*.

Steve Fielding, 2009
www.stevefielding.com

1

BEHIND CLOSED DOORS

William Smedley, 21 December 1875

'I have come to give myself up for murdering a woman named Elizabeth Firth I've been cohabiting with. I cut her throat with a razor in Orchard Street, and I have thrown the razor away on some slates near the factory on the iron bridge!'

As far as confessions went it was pretty comprehensive. Walking into Sheffield Town Hall police station, the man addressed Inspector Lawton, on duty at the front desk, and as good as placed a noose around his own neck.

Elizabeth 'Liz' Firth lived with her children in Orchard Street, Harvest Lane, Sheffield, and for several years had earned a living taking in washing for neighbours, one of whom was 50-year-old cutlery maker William Smedley. They were also often seen out together in one of the numerous public houses in that part of Sheffield, and as often as not Smedley would spend the night at her home.

On Friday evening, 27 August 1875, Smedley and Liz spent the evening together at the Harrow Inn. Later that night a neighbour standing on her doorstep saw the couple making their way home. They seemed to be in an intense discussion and as they approached their home, she heard Liz raise her voice and shout 'No!' to something Smedley had said. As the neighbour went back inside and closed her door she heard Liz repeat the word 'No!' followed by an emphatic 'Never!'

No sooner had she closed the door than there was a loud crash. Hurrying outside, the neighbour saw that Liz had fallen against her shutter and slumped to the ground, with blood gushing from a hideous throat wound. Smedley, whom she had recognised, made off in the opposite direction.

With the help of a neighbour Liz Firth was carried to a nearby public house and a doctor was sent for, but it was clear that the unfortunate woman was beyond help and she was declared dead once the doctor arrived. By this time Smedley had given himself up and was already in the police cells.

Investigating Smedley's confession, a constable went to the iron bridge mentioned and found the bloodstained razor. Interviewed the following morning, Smedley said, 'I am sorry for what I have done. I expect she is dead.' Told that she was, he simply bowed his head.

Smedley was arraigned for wilful murder at Leeds Assizes before Mr Justice Lindley on 2 December. Initially entering a plea of guilty, he claimed he did not know what he was doing at the time of the attack, but following legal advice he changed his plea to not guilty.

Smedley's defence sought to prove that he was insane at the time of the murder and that the crime had been committed whilst he was labouring under a fit of temporary homicidal mania. Contesting this, the prosecution called Inspector Lawson, who told the court that when Smedley had surrendered to him after the murder he had been eating a slice of bread and had seemed perfectly calm and collected.

The court also heard of the lack of motive and the fondness the prisoner felt for the deceased; but the prosecution contested any claims of insanity by claiming that the immediate confession proved that the killer knew what he had done was wrong.

The jury, without retiring, found Smedley guilty. Addressing the prisoner the judge spoke in slow sombre tones:

William Smedley, you have been convicted by the jury of the wilful murder of Elizabeth Firth, and I for one am bound to say that I think no twelve reasonable men could have come to any other conclusion that they did. I mean to say that there is really no evidence at all, upon which any reasonable man that could believe that you were or are insane. It is under those circumstances, my painful duty to pass sentence upon you.

Smedley was removed from the dock and taken to Armley Gaol, Leeds, by the Governor and a warder in a horse-drawn carriage.

It would be the first execution at the prison in over eleven years and the first behind closed doors. Eighteen days after sentence, Smedley, who told his guards he had committed the crime through jealousy, walked calmly to the gallows erected in the prison yard close to the hospital. Reporters noted that he trembled violently as Thomas Askern adjusted the noose, but death was reported to be instant.

2

HANGED TWICE

John Henry Johnson, 3 April 1877

John Johnson had found life in America a tough struggle following his emigration from Bradford in 1863. The former fent (cloth) dealer had stuck it out across the Atlantic for over a decade before he decided enough was enough and made plans to return to his native Bradford. With a promise to his wife and son, who were staying behind, that he would pay their fares when he had saved the money, in June 1876 he boarded a ship and returned home.

Arriving in Bradford, 37-year-old Johnson initially took lodgings on Wakefield Road, sharing a house with Amos Waite and Waite's girlfriend, Amelia Sewell. However, after just a few weeks, Amelia began a relationship with Johnson. Waite seemed to have accepted he had lost his girl to the other man, but as soon as he became drunk he would go into bouts of jealous rage. Johnson took new lodgings close to Waite's home and the men still saw each other in the many public houses that littered the surrounding area.

On Boxing Day 1876, Johnson, Waite and Amelia were drinking in the Bedford Arms on Wakefield Road. Johnson's brother joined them and it seemed relations between Waite and Johnson were cordial enough. Sometime during the afternoon Amelia left the bar and went to the ladies' toilet situated outside in the back yard. Waite followed, and, as she returned across the yard, he began to berate then assault her. Her screams alerted Johnson, who rushed to her aid and the two men fought until Johnson's brother intervened and escorted Johnson home.

Johnson arrived home and, once his brother had departed, he went upstairs to his room, picked up a revolver and returned to the Bedford Arms. As he approached the pub he saw Waite standing outside, and drawing the revolver from his pocket he addressed his erstwhile friend, 'Well, Amos, that will do for thee!' He then shot at him from point blank range, the bullet striking him in the heart and killing him instantly. Taken to the nearby police station Johnson had a violent epileptic fit, and, once he had recovered, he was charged with wilful murder.

At his trial before Mr Justice Lopes on Monday 12 March 1877, Johnson's defence was based around insanity. The court was told of his fit following the murder; that the prisoner suffered from epilepsy, and how his grandfather had died in the Wakefield Lunatic Asylum, but the prosecution showed clear motive for the shooting. They claimed the shooting was the result of a drunken quarrel between the two men rivalling for the affections of the woman, and the fact that Johnson did not have a gun with him earlier in the day, but returned with it after the quarrel, showed premeditation to commit murder and discounted a charge of manslaughter. It took the jury just twenty-five minutes to find the prisoner guilty as charged.

On the night before the execution, Johnson spent a restless night and did not undress for bed. At 6.30 a.m. on the fateful morning he took Holy Communion with the prison chaplain then ate a good breakfast. At 8.45 a.m., executioner Thomas Askern entered the cell with two warders and pinioned Johnson's arms. A procession led by the High Sheriff and Prison Governor formed and made its way to the scaffold, which had again been erected close to the prison hospital.

As Johnson mounted the scaffold the chaplain read passages from the burial service. The condemned man took his place on the trap and Askern placed the white bag over Johnson's head and secured the noose. 'Tell my mother I died happily,' Johnson said to the chaplain. It was to be painfully untrue.

Seeing all was ready, Askern pushed the lever and the trap opened. Johnson fell with a violent jerk but his weight proved too much for the hangman's rope, causing it to snap near the noose. As the condemned man crashed to the ground, clearly still alive, warders rushed forward and tore away the black calico curtain that shrouded the lower part of the scaffold.

Johnson lay dazed but uninjured, and was helped to a chair while above the scaffold the pale and shaken Askern swiftly procured a new, thicker rope and secured it around the beam. The wording of the law was that the prisoner was to be hanged by the neck until dead. This was usually done in one attempt, but despite the botched execution the law still had to be carried out and the prisoner sat in silence while the hangman made adjustments to the drop.

Ten minutes later, Johnson climbed the steps to the scaffold for a second time. Askern pulled the lever and Johnson fell just 3ft. This time the rope stayed taut and the prisoner struggled violently several times until almost five minutes had passed and the body was finally hanging still.

Thomas Askern, who had assured the Governor that he had tested his ropes before the execution, did not officiate at any further executions.

How the Illustrated Police News *recorded the botched execution of John Johnson. (T.J. Leech Archive)*

3

'FOR THAT I DONE BUT NEVER INTENDED'

Charles Frederick Peace, 25 February 1879

Charlie Peace was born in Sheffield in May 1832, the youngest son of a one-legged lion tamer. At the age of 14, while working in a factory, Peace almost lost his own leg when he was injured by a red-hot piece of iron, which pierced his leg and left him partially crippled for the rest of his life. He spent eighteen months in hospital with a further six months bed rest at home. To occupy his time he learned to play the violin, becoming so proficient he was able to earn money at it playing in pubs and clubs.

In 1851, Peace broke into the home of the mother of the Mayor of Sheffield, for which he received his first prison sentence: one month's hard labour. On his release he moved to Bradford, where he took up with two teenage girls; Emma James and Mary Neild, and in 1854 the three of them broke into premises in Sheffield, where they stole a large quantity of jewellery. Peace was soon arrested and sentenced to four years' imprisonment. Taken to Wakefield Gaol, he attempted to escape by clambering onto the roof of a house in the prison yard, removing slates and lowering himself into the bedroom below. The noise alerted warders who found Peace hiding on top of one of the wardrobes.

Released in 1858, a year later he married a widow, Mrs Hannah Ward, but was soon back in gaol, this time for six years, before he earned his freedom. With his wife now running a shop on Kenyan Street, Sheffield, Peace was reunited with her in 1864. He managed to stay out of gaol for a further two years before he was arrested during the course of a robbery and sentenced to eight years at the fearsome Portland Prison, where he led a revolt against the guards and received a flogging with the cat o' nine tails, and transportation to a prison fortress in Gibraltar. Serving the remainder of his sentence at Chatham, he was released on ticket of leave in August 1872 and for the next six years he kept out of trouble.

Peace and his wife went to live at Banner Cross Terrace in Sheffield. During the day he worked as a carpenter and picture framer, but by night he continued his work as an expert cat burglar. He was now 43 years old, although the harsh prison regimes he had endured left him looking at least ten years older. Standing just 5ft 4in tall, he was thin and wiry, and despite his disability he was still immensely strong and agile.

Peace soon struck up a friendship with next-door neighbours, civil engineer Arthur Dyson and his attractive wife Katherine. Peace soon became enamoured by Katherine and began calling on her so often that Dyson finally warned him to stay away and not to call at their house again. Peace responded by waving a pistol in Katherine Dyson's face and threatening to blow her brains out. The terrified woman contacted the police and a warrant was issued against Peace, who, fearing another spell in prison, fled with his family to Hull, where he opened a café. Peace still maintained his fascination with Katherine Dyson, and instructed his son-in-law, who remained in Sheffield, to keep him informed of any news of the couple.

By this time Peace had taken to travelling to other cities to continue his life of crime, and one place he visited regularly was Manchester. In August 1876 he was breaking into a house in the Whalley Range district of the city when two policemen spotted him climbing out of a window. The officers,

PCs Beanland and Cock, split up and as Peace made his escape he walked straight into PC Beanland. Peace managed to evade his clutches and as he vaulted a low garden wall he found himself face to face with the other officer. After a moment's hesitation, Peace whipped out a pistol and fired two shots. The first shot flew wide but the second hit the officer in the chest, fatally wounding him. Peace fled into the night and made his way back to Hull.

Police in Manchester soon rounded up a pair of suspects, brothers John and William Habron, and although both maintained their innocence they stood trial for the shooting of PC Nicholas Cock. John was later acquitted but 24-year-old William, with no alibi for the night of the murder, was convicted. Watching from the public gallery as the judge donned the black cap and passed sentence of death, was Charlie Peace.

Fortunately for the condemned man, and unusually in the case of the murder of a serving policeman, the Home Secretary showed mercy, and sentence on Habron was commuted to life imprisonment. On the evening of 28 November 1876, the day after Habron had been sentenced to death, Peace travelled to Sheffield and called on the Dysons. He hid in their yard until Mrs Dyson appeared at her back door and made her way to the outside toilet. Spotting Peace she locked herself inside and shouted for her husband. Dyson came outside and as he chased the unwelcome visitor down the street, Peace pulled out the same gun that had killed PC Cock. As Dyson was closing in, Peace fired two shots, the second hit Dyson in the head and he died from his wound two hours later.

Peace hurried back to Hull where he gathered up his family and fled overnight to London. Peace moved into a house at 5 East Terrace, Peckham, and set about disguising himself. He began wearing spectacles, shaved off his beard and altered the colour of his face by staining it with walnut juice. To complete his disguise he adopted the name John Thompson and moved his mistress into the upstairs part of the house while his wife took over the basement. Back in Yorkshire, a coroner's court brought in a verdict of wilful murder against Charles Peace and police launched a hunt for the killer, with a reward of £100 offered for information leading to his arrest.

For two years Peace worked by day in the workshop adjacent to his house, tinkering with inventions and making picture frames, while at night he brought his one man crime wave to the streets of South London. Then, on 9 October 1878, he committed his last burglary. Having broken into a house in Blackheath, Peace was stacking pieces of silver onto a table ready for removal when a passing policeman noticed a light flickering in the drawing room of the house. He called for assistance and with two other officers covering the rear of the house he knocked on the front door and rang the bell. Peace tried to flee via the window as the officer gave chase. Cornered at the bottom of the garden, Peace pulled out his gun and ordered the policeman to 'Keep back or by God I will shoot you!'

Undeterred the policeman advanced. Peace fired four shots; they all missed. The officer then punched him to the ground, whereupon Peace aimed again and shouted, 'You bugger, I'll settle you this time!' This time the officer was wounded in the arm, but by now the shooting had alerted his colleagues and together they were able to detain the gunman.

After a terrific struggle, Peace was finally arrested and charged with attempted murder. He gave his name as John Ward and before Mr Justice Hawkins at the Old Bailey in November 1878 he was sentenced to life imprisonment and taken to Pentonville Prison.

With Peace safely behind bars his mistress sought to claim the reward money offered by Yorkshire Police. She contacted officers in Sheffield and informed them that John Ward serving life in Pentonville was in fact fugitive Charles Frederick Peace. On 22 January 1879, Peace was escorted from his cell at Pentonville and taken by train from Kings Cross to Sheffield. Reaching the outskirts of the city, and as the express began to slow down, Peace made one last desperate bid for freedom. He momentarily distracted the guard before hurling himself head first through the train window. For almost two miles the warder clung to his ankles until Peace was able to free himself from the grip and tumble to the tracks. Although he suffered a heavy fall, Peace somehow escaped serious injury and was taken to Sheffield, where an angry crowd hissed as he was led inside.

Police photograph of John Ward, aka Charlie Peace. (T.J. Leech Archive)

The execution of Charlie Peace, as sketched by the Illustrated Police News. (T.J. Leech Archive)

Hangman William Marwood made three visits to Leeds Prison. (Author's collection)

Charles Peace stood trial for the murder of Arthur Dyson before Mr Justice Lopes at the Leeds Assizes on 4 February 1879. The evidence against him was strong and it took the jury just ten minutes to return their verdict.

Awaiting execution, Peace made one last honourable gesture. He asked to speak to the vicar of Darnall, the parish close to where Peace had lived at Banner Cross, Sheffield. During the interview Peace confessed to the murder of PC Cock in 1876:

> People will say that I was a hardened wretch for allowing an innocent man to suffer for the crime of which I was guilty, but what man would have given himself up under such circumstances knowing as I

did that I should certainly be hanged? Now that I am going to forfeit my own life and feel that I have nothing to gain by further secrecy, I think it is right in the sight of God and man to clear this innocent young man.

In his last meeting with his wife, Peace gave her a funeral card that read: 'In Memory of Charles Peace who was executed in Armley Prison Tuesday February 25th, 1879 Aged 47, for that I done but never intended.'

Tuesday 25 February 1879 was a bitterly cold day and the ground was covered with a layer of snow when, at 8 a.m., Peace was escorted to the gallows. Four reporters were present at the execution and took notes as Peace made a short speech stating that his last thoughts were for his children and their mother. William Marwood waited patiently for him to finish talking before placing the hood and noose and deftly pushing the lever.

Peace died unaware that his mistress had applied for the £100 reward offered for his capture. William Habron was given a free pardon and released with £800 payment in compensation.

4

DRUNKEN PASSION

James Hall, 23 May 1881

Shortly before midnight on Saturday 26 March 1881, Selina Hall and her boyfriend made their way home from a public house in Sheffield city centre. Reaching the house they shared with Selina's parents on Shelf Street, they were unable to gain entry as the door was locked and barred. Looking through the window, they saw Selina's father standing over her mother holding a hatchet. After the young couple shouted and banged on the window, her father, James Hall, a 53-year-old unemployed cutler, eventually opened the door.

'What are you up to with the door fastened?' Selina asked, to which Hall replied, 'I'll show thee what I'm doing,' and struck his daughter in the face with the axe. Fortunately the blow just grazed her chin, and as Selina rushed down the street screaming, her boyfriend managed to overpower Hall, while a neighbour, who had been attracted by the commotion, called the police. Arriving at the scene they found the body of 48-year-old Mary Ann 'Polly' Hall.

Taken into custody, Hall confessed to the murder of his wife and explained his motive. He claimed that three years earlier he had come home from work unexpectedly and found his wife with another man. He later forgave her but had warned that if she were ever unfaithful again he would kill her. At 11 p.m. on the night of the crime, he came home from the pub sooner than usual and found his wife on the sofa with a neighbour, William Lowe. Mrs Hall grappled with her husband while the neighbour made his escape. Then, in a violent, drunken rage, Hall picked up a hatchet and attacked her.

At Hall's trial before Mr Justice Kay on 6 May, Selina Hall denied that her mother was an adulteress, as did William Lowe, who claimed he was nowhere near the house on the night of the murder. Hall's defence counsel claimed that at the time of the attack Hall was driven insane by drink and jealousy, and was not, therefore, guilty of murder. The judge dismissed this, adding that drunken jealousy was no excuse for murder.

5

CRUELTY AT SEA

Osmond Otto Brand, 23 May 1882

'Skipper, my sister Emma knows you.' It was an innocent remark, made without malice by a young boy to the skipper of the boat they were about to set sail on. Yet it was to have dire consequences.

On Friday 16 December 1881, the sailing packet *Royal Sun* slipped out of Hull's Albert Dock and headed out to sea. Skippered by co-owner 28-year-old Osmond Otto Brand, it contained just a crew of five, including 14-year-old apprentice William Papper. While on shore leave, Papper had, for the last two years, lodged with the skipper and it was as they had prepared to set to sea that he had made the seemingly innocuous remark.

Unbeknown to Papper, not only did the skipper know his sister Emma, but he had been carrying on an affair with her. As the remark had been made in the presence of Brand's wife, he flew into a rage and swore he would make the boy pay for his loose talk.

Brand was something of a brute and often bullied the crew if he felt they were not pulling their weight. Once the boat had left port he began a tirade of abuse against the youngster. That night, as they anchored off Sunk Island in the mouth of the Humber, Brand attacked Papper with a rope, whipping him across the hands and face. He continued the beatings on a daily basis, telling the crew it was punishment for failing to do his duties and for putting all their lives in danger.

Throughout the voyage, the punishments and beating became crueller. Papper was refused food – given just a broken biscuit to eat – and made to crawl out onto the bowsprit in choppy seas while the crew threw buckets of icy water over him. When he was allowed back on deck, the skipper told Papper he was going to be hanged. A rope was thrown around a beam, fastened around Papper's neck and he was winched off the ground. The beam snapped under the boy's weight and, in a rage, he was kicked unconscious by the brutal skipper. It seemed the crew were too terrified to intervene, but while the captain was occupied with other matters some of the men tended to the boy, giving him hot tea and cleaning his wounds.

The punishments continued: Papper was now forced to live on deck at the mercy of the elements. The December wind and cold made for a harrowing few days and as Christmas Day arrived, while the crew enjoyed a feast in the warm galley below, he was served the remains of the ship's dog's dinner.

It was perhaps a merciful release for the wretched youth when, on 29 December, after having excrement rubbed in his face, Papper was pushed down into the bilge hold where Brand jumped up and down on his prone body. The boy was finally taken below and placed in a bunk, where he died from his injuries that night. Brand tossed the boy's body overboard and then turned on his crew, warning them that they were all in this together and that they should concoct a cover story.

When the boat returned to port on 15 January 1882, Brand informed Papper's parents that their son had been involved in a tragic accident and had been washed overboard. The matter was reported to the police, who were initially satisfied by the skipper's account, only to open a murder investigation when two of the crew decided to contact the authorities.

Based on the testimony of the crew, Brand, along with all the crew, was taken into custody, where charges were then made against the skipper and Frederick Ryecroft, who was alleged to have thrown the boy into the bilge. The remainder of the crew were released, but ordered to make statements about the behaviour of the skipper during that fateful voyage.

The key players in the brutal murder of William Papper. (Author's collection)

Brand was originally scheduled to stand trial at Hull, but as feelings against the skipper were so high it was felt they would be unable to find an unbiased jury and it was decided that it should take place at Leeds. Brand and Ryecroft appeared before Mr Justice Williams on 4 May. Ryecroft pleaded guilty to a charge of common assault and was sentenced to three months imprisonment; Brand, faced with the testimonies of the crew, was found guilty of murder and sentenced to death.

As he was transported from the court to Armley Gaol by horse-drawn cab, the skipper made an attempt to escape, only to be thwarted by the Prison Governor and a warder. Three weeks later William Papper was avenged.

6

'ALL THROUGH DRINK'

Joseph Laycock, 26 August 1884

'Oh my children, my children. Lord have mercy on my children.'
Last words of Joseph Laycock, 26 August 1884

Thirty-four-year-old ex-soldier turned hawker and petty crook Joseph Laycock lived with his pregnant wife Maria and their four children at White Croft, Sheffield. At 6 p.m. on 10 July 1884, Laycock, who had just completed a three-week stint in prison, complained to a police constable that his wife was out drinking with another man. The officer could see that Laycock was sober but told him there was nothing the police could do to interfere in such matters.

Laycock returned home and at about 10 p.m. that night he and his wife sat down to supper. They had since patched up their quarrel and he asked her to share a drink with him. When she refused he became angry and said, 'You might as well have some while you have the chance; it will be the last time you have the chance!'

Later that night neighbours heard a scream, and when they went to investigate they discovered the body of 25-year-old Maria Laycock lying on the floor in the kitchen. Her throat had been cut. Upstairs an even more horrific sight greeted them: on the floor in one of the bedrooms lay the bodies of four young children, aged between 8 and 2, each with its throat cut. Beside them on the bedroom floor was their father, a large bloodstained table knife in his hands, also with his throat cut. But, unlike the wounds on his wife and children, Laycock's weren't fatal.

'Good God, what have you done?' cried a neighbour.

Laycock made no reply, simply placing his finger to his lips and pleading, 'Let me die.' Rushed to hospital, Laycock maintained his death wish. 'Cut my throat deeper,' he begged the surgeon attending his wounds.

On Monday 14 July, the five victims were buried in pauper's graves at Intake Cemetery, following a procession through the city watched by crowds estimated at over 25,000. By 25 July Laycock was sufficiently recovered to face the coroner's inquest. Charged with murdering his wife and four children, he replied in a hushed voice, 'It was all through drink; it was about midnight when I did it.'

At his trial before Mr Justice Mathew in early August, Laycock's defence claimed that he was not at the time responsible for his acts. The court heard that Laycock was very fond of his children, but had been in trouble several times for assaults, the latest, shortly before the murders, for an assault on his wife.

The court heard evidence of insanity on behalf of the prisoner: his maternal grandfather and his father had both drowned themselves and two uncles had committed suicide, one by cutting his throat, the other by throwing himself before a steam train.

Throughout the trial Laycock expressed remorse, sobbing bitterly and begging forgiveness, but to no avail. He claimed that on the night of the tragedy he had resolved to kill himself, and went to kiss

Bolton hangman James Billington carried out his first execution at Leeds when he hanged Joseph Laycock in 1884. (Author's collection)

the children for the last time. On going downstairs his wife taunted him to such an extent that he became overcome by madness.

Following conviction, he made a statement blaming his mother-in-law for the tragedy, claiming she encouraged his wife to go out drinking to the extent that she would often return home unfit to look after either him or the children.

His execution marked the debut of a new hangman, James Billington of Farnworth, Bolton. Laycock spent his last moments awaiting the hangman in terror. He was crying as Billington entered the condemned cell and asked pitifully, 'You will not hurt me?'

'No, tha'll nivver feel it, for tha'll be out of existence i'two minutes,' Billington re-assured him as he adjusted the pinion straps. Laycock then fainted but was revived by warders and escorted to the scaffold. As the noose was being tightened around his neck, he spoke for the last time, asking the Lord to look after his children.

7

'A BONNY MESS IN THAT HOUSE!'

Henry Hobson, 22 August 1887

On the morning of 23 July 1887, Mrs Ada Stothard, the 22-year-old wife of a wealthy Sheffield engineer, was having morning coffee with her maid in the kitchen at their home at 99 Montague Street, when there was a call at the house. She recognised the caller as 54-year-old Henry Hobson, a former caretaker and engine-tenter at the family's Horn Works who had been dismissed in the previous year for drunkenness, but she opened the door and asked what he wanted.

Hobson said he was just passing, and after informing them that he had set up as a rag-and-bone man he asked if he could have a drink of water. His request granted he left, only to return fifteen minutes later, this time asking for a piece of cord. No sooner had Mrs Stothard gone to search for some in the cellar, Hobson took out a knife and attacked the maid, Florence Mosley, cutting her on the neck and shoulder. Her screams attracted the attention of Mrs Stothard, who came running up from the cellar to investigate. As soon as she appeared Hobson turned on her, while the maid rushed into the street screaming, 'Murder!'

Hobson took flight, passing a couple in a nearby alleyway and telling them that there had been 'a bonny mess in that house!' Ada had been wounded in the neck, and, although she was still on her feet when help arrived, she collapsed to the floor with blood spurting from a horrific wound. Within minutes she had bled to death.

John Stothard was contacted at work and notified of the murderous attack on his wife and the identity of her attacker. He rounded up a number of his employees who all knew Hobson by sight and a hunt for the attacker began.

Later that afternoon a police officer spotted Hobson on Furnival Road in the city and he was taken into custody. A knife was found in his pockets and his clothing was bloodstained. Placed on an identity parade, he was identified by the two men he had passed in the alley as he fled the murder scene, and later that day he was charged with the attempted murder of Florence Mosley and the wilful murder of Ada Stothard.

At his Leeds Assizes trial before Mr Justice Mathew, on 5 August, just thirteen days after the murder, Hobson pleaded not guilty. The prosecution alleged that he had cut Mrs Stothard's throat as revenge for being dismissed from his job at the family firm, and it took the jury a little over ten minutes to agree.

Awaiting execution, Hobson told his guards he wasn't afraid to face the hangman, stating that, 'the sooner he comes, the longer will be my rest!'

8

THE UNLUCKY ONE

James William Richardson, 22 May 1888

James Richardson had worked as a labourer at Messrs Humphrey and Chamberlain's brick and carbon works in Barnsley for five years, when he was suddenly dismissed for misconduct. On 21 March 1888, 23-year-old Richardson had been tasked to work in the carbon factory on a grinding machine and while he was sweeping away some of the dust his brush got caught in the rollers and was damaged beyond repair.

When foreman William Berridge saw the damaged broom he accused Richardson of deliberately breaking it and began to berate him in front of the workforce. After several minutes of quarrelling, Richardson threw down his tools and demanded his wages. Berridge refused to hand them over as he also did to Richardson's request for them to be given to his friend who also worked at the factory, telling him that he would have to return later to collect his money from the wages office.

Richardson went home and told his wife he had been dismissed. She was supportive, telling him the job was dirty and hard work and he would have no trouble finding a new position. He then ate breakfast and decided to collect his wages, slipping into his jacket pocket a revolver he had purchased in the previous year and which he was hoping to pawn to raise some extra money.

Shortly before lunch he returned to the factory and asked to see Frank Chamberlain, the manager. Told he was busy, Richardson waited outside an office and, looking through the window, he saw that Berridge was talking to Chamberlain. Berridge saw Richardson and began laughing with the manager and at the same time he pulled out his tongue and gesticulated at him.

After fifteen minutes, Berridge came out of the office and hissed at Richardson, gently elbowing him in the stomach as he passed. The foreman walked on a few yards when Richardson pulled out his revolver and fired three times at Berridge before rushing out into the street. Chamberlain followed him outside and shouted for him to stop. Richardson carried on until he reached the end of the street, where he stopped in his tracks and cried, 'What have I done?'

Initially held on a charge of attempted murder, this was changed to wilful murder when the foreman died from his wounds a week later. Richardson was tried before Mr Justice Mathew at Leeds Assizes on 3 May. Despite a spirited defence by his counsel on grounds of provocation, the fact that he had collected a gun from home and returned to the factory suggested otherwise. Justice Mathew, feared on the assize circuit and dubbed 'the Hanging Judge', made it clear what he thought the verdict should be and summed up heavily against the defendant.

That spring sitting of Leeds Assizes was one of the busiest for years, and ended with four people being sentenced to death, no doubt to the delight of Mr Justice Mathew. Delight soon turned to shock when one prisoner was reprieved immediately on account of a flaw in the judge's summing up. In the meantime the hangman was engaged to carry out the remaining three executions at the prison. A woman named Mary Holliday, who had murdered her 9-year-old daughter at Driffield, was to be hanged on Monday 21 May; while a Dr William Burke from Barnsley, who had shot his 9-year-old daughter at Monk Bretton, was due to be hanged alongside Richardson on the Tuesday.

When Billington arrived at the prison on Sunday afternoon, he learned that both Holliday and Burke had been granted reprieves, again based on the biased summing up by the trial judge. With this in mind, a vigorous campaign for a respite for Richardson was launched. It was not to be and Richardson, the unlucky one in the Home Office lottery of reprieves, went to the gallows on a bright sunny morning, having left a touching farewell note to his wife pledging his love for her, and promising that he would await her on the other side.

9

'I DONE FOR HER, I'LL SWING FOR HER'

Charles Bulmer, 1 January 1889

Stableman Charles Bulmer had been unhappily married to his wife, Elizabeth, for the last dozen or so years until finally, in the autumn of 1888, matters reached a head. The couple came to blows and as a result he was bound over to keep the peace, and soon afterwards they decided to separate for good. After moving out of the family home at Lockwood, Huddersfield, Bulmer found lodgings, but returned on Monday 10 September to collect the remainder of his possessions.

Mrs Bulmer refused entry on account of him being drunk and abusive. A neighbour heard them quarrelling, and when he later called at the house he discovered Elizabeth lying on the kitchen floor with her throat cut so severely that her head had almost been severed.

The hunt for the killer was a short one. Following the murder, Bulmer had gone to see a friend where he had washed the blood from his hands and said he was going to give himself up. 'I done for her, I'll swing for her,' he said, before setting off to find a policeman.

On Thursday 13 December, Bulmer found himself before Mr Justice Baron Pollock at Leeds Assizes. The case hinged around the issues of insanity and premeditation. When Bulmer had gave himself up he had blamed the crime on drink, and the defence sought to claim he was insane by virtue of being unaware of what he was doing as he was too drunk. They pointed to evidence given by one witness who had travelled back to Lockwood with Bulmer on the night of the murder. They had shared a railway carriage and talk was of the most recent Jack the Ripper murder in London. Bulmer had made several references to the murders and to what it must be like to face the hangman. This, the prosecution alleged, showed that his thinking wasn't rational and suggested insanity.

This was easily disputed by the prosecution, who pointed out that Bulmer had told a friend soon after the murder that he was prepared to 'swing for what he had done', which surely showed that he was aware of his actions. They also suggested a motive when it was discovered that Bulmer had killed his wife after she accused him of having an affair with another woman and that she was using this to secure a divorce from him.

Hangman James Billington spent the last day of 1888 in the confines of Armley Gaol, preparing the gallows and missing the New Year's Eve celebrations taking place across the country. At 8 a.m. the following morning, Charles Bulmer, who three months earlier had speculated to others what he thought it would be like to face the hangman, discovered those feelings first hand as he was led to the scaffold and hanged.

10

'ACTING AT JACK THE RIPPER!'

Frederick Brett, 31 December 1889

Early in 1889, Manchester-born Frederick Brett, a 39-year-old railway labourer, and his wife of two years, 40-year-old Margaret, moved across the Pennines to Halifax where he secured work on the new high-level railway. The former army reservist soon changed occupations and found a position as a brickyard labourer at Elland Edge, but they continued to live in lodgings at Mile Thorn Yard in the town.

Although a hard-working man, Brett was also a heavy drinker and his drinking caused him to harbour unfounded suspicions that his wife was being just a little too friendly with some of his workmates. She repeatedly denied that anything untoward had occurred, but he continued to harbour jealous thoughts against her.

On Saturday night, 19 October, the couple had been out drinking. When they returned home, Brett was rather the worse for drink and turned on his wife, pleading, 'Maggie, you seem to treat me so lightly. If you don't want me say so and I will go at once.'

As before, she reassured him his suspicions were ungrounded and told him to come up to bed.

On the following afternoon they were drinking in the parlour with their landlord, James Hindley, an old man who ran the boarding house since his retirement. Since rising for breakfast, relations between Brett and his wife had cooled and it was later claimed they had spent the night quarrelling in their room. After finishing his drink Brett asked his wife to join him in their room. She initially refused, only to relent when his pleadings began to cause her embarrassment in front of the landlord. No sooner had she closed the door then sounds of a struggle were heard. 'Jim! Jim help!' she cried, but by the time the old man climbed the stairs Maggie Brett was lying still on the bed, with a terrible gash to her throat. Brett stood with a bloodstained pruning knife in his hand and made no attempt to deny his guilt. As one of the lodgers rushed to notify the police, Brett went downstairs and sat at the kitchen table smoking a pipe, waiting to be taken into custody.

'Yes, I have done it and it can't be undone,' he told the startled police officer who took him into custody. 'I was only acting at Jack the Ripper!'

Brett offered a defence of insanity through drink when he appeared before Mr Justice Manisty at West Riding Assizes in December. The prosecution simply claimed he had committed the brutal attack through jealousy and deserved the full rigour of the law. The jury took just a short time to concur and Brett was duly hanged on 31 December 1889.

11

'BLAME YOURSELF AND LEICESTER JACK'

Robert West, 31 December 1889

Dawn was breaking over the fairground at Sheffield, when, in his caravan, travelling showman Thomas Twigdon, in town for the annual Handsworth Woodhouse Feast, was roused from his sleep by a persistent rapping on the door of his van. It was Saturday 17 August 1889, and looking at his watch he saw it was almost 5.30 a.m. Rubbing sleep from his eyes he asked who was there.

'Tom, I have got something to tell you,' a man whispered.

The bleary-eyed showman opened the door to be greeted by fellow traveller, 45-year-old Robert West, standing on the steps.

'Come to the police station. I've killed my wife,' he said simply.

Twigdon dressed and, in the company of another traveller woken by the noise, ventured into West's caravan. The body of 31-year-old Emma West was lying on the bed with a huge gash in her throat. West's 9-year-old child was still fast asleep next to its dead mother and amongst the bedclothes was a large kitchen knife, which West said he had used to kill his wife.

At the inquest held a few days later, West claimed that he and his wife had previously been very happy and had not had a cross word until trouble started a few months before. Mrs Emma Sketchley, the victim's mother, disputed this claim, shouting, 'But you had. You bad man, you murderer, you ought to have your neck stretched!'

'Blame yourself and Leicester Jack, not me,' West countered, adding, 'I have done it and I am very glad of it. I told you a long time while ago I should do it.'

Four months later, a pale-faced and dejected looking Robert West sat with his head in his hands in the dock before Mr Justice Manisty at the West Riding Assizes. There was no doubt that West was guilty of the murder of his wife, so the defence tried to show that the prisoner was insane at the time of the murder.

It was claimed that West had suffered a bad attack of brain fever some eight years before and he was warned to avoid drink. It was also shown that there was a history of insanity in the family. The Wests had been living happily enough together until the previous year, when he suspected his wife had began an affair with 30-year-old John Baines, better known as Leicester Jack, who ran a swings and coconut shy stall at various fairgrounds across the country.

The defence claimed that as a result of her suspected infidelity (which Baines strenuously denied in court) West had taken to drinking, which had led him to lose his temper and murder his wife.

In summing up, the judge told the jury that although there was evidence of insanity in the family, since his arrest West had shown no signs of insanity, and drunkenness could not be an excuse to commit a murder. After a short retirement the jury found him guilty but added a strong recommendation for mercy. He was hanged alongside Frederick Brett (*see* Chapter 10) in the first double execution carried out in private at the gaol.

12

ON ACCOUNT OF THE PROVOCATION

James Harrison, 26 August 1890

Thirty-six year-old James Harrison lived with his wife Hannah, their three children, and his 80-year-old mother, Bella Duckworth, in a small one-bedroom house at 7 Lord Street, near Bowling Station, Bradford. Like many people in the area, they were living barely above the poverty line when, in March 1890, Harrison was made redundant from his job as a dyer's labourer. The family became dependant on the money earned by Hannah and the children in the local mills, occasionally assisted by items of food given to them by Harrison's sister. Although the gifts given by his sister may have helped them while he was out of work, to his wife they were a cause of anger and resentment, and she scornfully mocked them as charity. She also felt that Harrison was relying on these gifts a little too much instead of finding work himself.

On Sunday night, 11 May, matters came to a head when Harrison returned from a night drinking in the pub. On the previous day his sister had given him a piece of meat and when he returned home that night he asked his wife to cook it for them. Instead of doing as she was asked, Hannah Harrison flew into a rage. She was unhappy that she and the children went out to work while he chose to idle around at home and, refusing to cook the meat, she called him a 'lazy bastard' and went upstairs to bed.

James Harrison and his wife. (T.J. Leech Archive)

At 5 a.m. the following morning, Harrison rose and went downstairs to prepare a fire. He was still seething about what his wife had said on the previous evening. His mother was already up and she saw him pick up a carving knife and return upstairs. He woke his wife, and when she saw the knife in his hand she pleaded for mercy. She was able to knock the knife from his hand as the children ran downstairs screaming for help. Harrison then picked up the poker from beside the bedroom fireplace and battered his wife about the head until she was dead.

At his trial at West Riding Assizes before Mr Justice Charles on 6 August, he pleaded guilty through extreme provocation. The defence asked for a verdict of manslaughter, claiming that Harrison was a good father and husband, and until he lost his job he was an easygoing and hard-working man, who was kind to his wife and mother, always giving them money when he received his wages. His wife, on the other hand, was a quick-tempered brute, who would beat the children without warning and would often provoke her husband into violence.

The prosecution claimed that Harrison had brutally murdered his wife after she had scorned him and refused to cook his supper on the previous evening. In front of their children she had pleaded for him to 'spare her for the sake of the children', but he had cruelly and brutally slain her and deserved the full penalty of the law. The jury agreed, but recommended him to mercy on account of the provocation.

13

A MOTHER'S DUTY

Walter Lewis Turner, 18 August 1891

On 6 June 1891, 6-year-old Barbara Waterhouse disappeared while playing outside her home at Horsforth, Leeds. Despite an intensive and frantic search of the area, police could find no sign of her.

Four days later, at a few minutes to midnight, PC Willis Moss, on duty in Alexander Street, close to the Town Hall, noticed a bundle wrapped in a shawl lying in a doorway. On closer examination he discovered it was the horrifically mutilated body of a young girl.

Identified as missing Barbara Woodhouse, a post-mortem found the child's throat had been cut with such force the head was almost severed and there was a large cut down the chest. Beside the hideous throat wounds, the body contained over forty stab wounds and had been completely drained of blood.

As detectives turned the hunt for a missing child into a murder enquiry, across the city Mrs Mary Cotterill had been told a fascinating story during a visit by her friend, 52-year-old Mrs Ann Turner and her 32-year-old son, Walter. Shortly before the body had been discovered, the Turners had visited the Cotterills and told them they had been shocked to find a trunk in the coal cellar at their home on Beck Lane, Horsforth, and when they opened it they found it contained the body of a young girl. They were advised to go the police at once, and when the Cotterills read about the murder in the following day's newspaper they were surprised to find no mention of the Turners.

Mr Cotterill became suspicious of his wife's friend and her son, and wrote to the police outlining his suspicions. In the meantime, detectives had already visited the Turners when the shawl was identified as being similar to one Ann Turner wore. Walter Turner's behaviour aroused suspicion and he was taken into custody.

'Prove it,' he taunted officers when told they interviewed him. Turner denied murdering the child and claimed that a quarryman called 'Jack' had asked him to dispose of the trunk. The following day, his mother confessed that she had helped her son dispose of the body.

They were tried separately before Mr Justice Grantham at Leeds Assizes. On Thursday 30 July, Ann Turner pleaded guilty to being an accessory to murder and was sentenced to life imprisonment. The following day, before a new jury, her son stood trial for murder. He pleaded not guilty. The prosecution claimed that Turner had committed a wicked, brutal murder, and their case was supported by evidence given by Turner's mother. She said that she had discovered the bundle in their home and suspected her son of being involved. He told her he wasn't and she felt it was a mother's duty to help her son. She only discovered that he had committed the murder following their arrest. She was entitled to refuse to testify against her son, but she chose to go into court and her evidence helped convict a brutal murderer.

The following day, Mr Justice Grantham announced that as a reward for her giving evidence, he was reducing Ann Turner's sentence to twelve month's penal servitude.

Walter Turner was taken to the death cell at Leeds where, a few days before his execution, he received a letter from his mother, serving her sentence at Wakefield Gaol:

Mr dear, dear Lu,
With deepest love and sympathy I write these words… my dear boy let me beg you to seek forgiveness from Him on high and may God in his mercy give you comfort and support and that we may meet again where sin and sorrow never come…
Your ever loving and affectionate mother
Ann Turner

Turner maintained his innocence following conviction, and on the night before his execution he made a detailed statement again blaming the mystery man, 'Jack', whom he claimed had left the body at his house after they had been drinking together. When Turner awoke he discovered the body, and fearful nobody would believe his innocence, he chose to dispose of it. He said he deeply regretted it, but maintained his innocence.

Turner was hanged in the new execution shed erected 15 yards from the condemned cell in the prison grounds. It also had a pit dug beneath it, removing the need for the prisoner to mount steps to reach the gallows, and thus speeded up proceedings.

Walter Turner and his mother, Ann. (Author's collection)

14

THE LINTHWAITE MURDER

James Stockwell, 5 January 1892

At 2 p.m. on Friday afternoon, 21 August 1891, widow Mrs Margaret Brooke, landlady of the Ivy Bridge public house at Milne Bridge, near Huddersfield, went into town, leaving the running of the bar in the hands of her waitress, Catherine 'Kate' Dennis, a 16-year-old Irish girl. The only customer at the time was a 32-year-old local man, James Stockwell, who was sitting in the kitchen eating a pie.

At 3 p.m. customer John Iredale entered the bar and stayed for fifteen minutes, thinking he was the only person apart from the girl in the building. As he left, he passed two men and saw them enter the pub. An hour or so later, David Beevers, a butcher's boy, called to deliver some meat and found the door locked. Alarmed at this, he called on a neighbour and between them they forced entry and found Kate dead on the floor. She had been stabbed in the neck and her clothing re-arranged as if she had been sexually assaulted.

On hearing about the murder, John Iredale contacted the police and told them about the two men he had seen enter the pub. He was able to give a good description of them and they were soon picked up on suspicion of the murder. Although one of them was carrying a knife, both were able to satisfy detectives of their innocence. Under questioning, Mrs Brooks recalled that James Stockwell had been in the kitchen when she left to go shopping, and when police went to interview him they discovered he had vanished.

Stockwell remained at liberty for sixteen days, hiding on the moors, foraging for food and surviving on herbs and scraps he could find in the fields. His spirit broken, he decided to seek help from his mother and crept into her house in the early hours desperate for food. He was arrested that morning and claimed he was tired of running and had chose to surrender. On remand at Wakefield Gaol, he was alleged to have confessed to a fellow inmate that he had committed the murder and that he hadn't eaten for over two weeks.

At his trial at Leeds Assizes before Mr Justice Wright on 15 December, Stockwell claimed that the girl had caused him to lose his temper by repeatedly pulling his hair as he lay asleep on a bench in the kitchen. In a rage, he had picked up the knife he had been eating his pie with and stabbed her in the neck.

Linthwaite murderer James Stockwell. (Author's Collection)

His defence was based on insanity, and the court heard that Stockwell's family had a history of insanity: his sister, mother and grandmother were or had been inmates in an asylum, and three uncles had all died in asylums.

The prosecution disputed the claims of insanity, pointing out that it was suggested that Stockwell had also made a sexual assault on the girl following the attack, and that running away after the murder proved that he knew what he had done was wrong. Following his conviction, Stockwell confessed to the chaplain prior to his execution that he was guilty of the murder.

The story has a sad footnote. On hearing that her daughter had been murdered, Kate Dennis's mother lost all sense of reasoning and was committed to an asylum. She died a few days before Stockwell walked to the gallows.

15

'NOW NO ONE ELSE CAN HAVE HER'

Henry Pickering, 14 June 1892

'It's no use roaring, as it won't mend it. It's done and can't be undone. I want naught but the rope, and I know I shall hang.'

Confession made by Henry Pickering following his arrest, April 1892

Twenty-nine-year-old Henry Pickering was a mechanic by trade, but since getting married in January 1892 he had been either unable or unwilling to find work. As a result, he and his wife Jane, a 23-year-old weaver, were unable to afford their own home and had to live with his parents at their home on Czar Street, Holbeck, Leeds. His refusal to find work also caused a strain on the relationship and the couple frequently quarrelled.

On Tuesday 19 April, Pickering purchased a carving knife from a hardware shop on Vicar Lane and asked the shopkeeper if it was sharp and ready for use. On the following Saturday, the Pickerings were at home with Henry's parents, Thomas and Matilda Pickering, and a son-in-law, when at soon after 10 p.m. Jane Pickering retired to bed. All were perfectly sober at the time. Henry Pickering followed his wife upstairs and moment's later sounds of a struggle were heard.

Thomas Pickering rushed upstairs and dragged his son from the room by his collar and pushed him downstairs. As the others went to tend to Jane, Henry Pickering rushed from the house. The scene inside the bedroom was ghastly. Jane Pickering lay in a pool of blood on the bed; her head almost severed from her body by a horrific wound to her throat, caused by the large carving knife left beside the body.

As the police were called and a manhunt began, Pickering was discovered hiding in a closet a few streets away and immediately confessed, telling police he was prepared to hang for his crime.

At his trial before Mr Justice Charles at Leeds Assizes on Tuesday 26 May, Pickering pleaded guilty when he first appeared in the dock. At the request of the judge, the prisoner was removed from the dock and, following a brief consultation with his advisors, he returned to the dock and this time pleaded not guilty.

The prosecution's case was formed mainly on the confession Pickering had made following his arrest. He had told officers that he had planned to kill his wife for several months, and that he had planned to cut his own throat before his father had intervened. Pickering claimed he had killed his wife after she told him she planned to leave him, and that 'now no one else can have her.'

The jury took just ten minutes to reach their verdict and once the black cap had been donned on the judge's wig and sentence passed, Pickering shouted 'hear, hear,' before being ushered from the dock.

16

ON A LONELY ROAD

Moses Cudworth, 18 August 1892

Showing his sister his bloodstained hands, Moses Cudworth made a shocking admission, 'This is Liza's blood, I've killed her!'

At lunchtime on Saturday 4 June 1892, Cudworth, a 40-year-old weaver from Earby, Skipton, and his 41-year-old wife Eliza, clocked off from their shifts at the same mill and stopped off for a pint of beer. They then returned home where, after collecting her 4-year-old daughter, Eliza Cudworth then set out off up Old Lane, towards Barnoldswick, to purchase the child a pair of clogs.

After watching his wife walk off up the quiet country lane, Cudworth waited ten minutes then spoke to his sister-in-law, Ellen Fitton, asking her if she had seen Eliza. Told she hadn't, he said he was going to look for her, but instead went to a friend's house and asked if he had any drink. Told he didn't, Cudworth left only to return a few minutes later and, throwing 2s on the table, asked them to fetch him a gallon of ale which he would drink while he waited for 'them' to come for him.

Ellen Fitton soon joined them at the house and it was then that Cudworth showed her his bloodstained hands and told her to call the police. As the police were summoned Ellen set off in search for Eliza and soon came across a man standing beside her body. She had been battered to death with a large stone that lay covered in blood beside the body.

At his trial before Mr Justice Grantham on Thursday 28 July, the prosecution stated that the motive for the crime was jealousy. They pointed to the fact that Cudworth had suspected his wife had been unfaithful with their lodger in the previous year and, following a quarrel, the lodger was asked to leave the house.

On his arrest, Cudworth had confessed that he had followed Eliza as she set off to purchase clogs and he had asked her for some money to buy drink. When she refused, he picked up a large stone and battered her to death. He said that he was drunk at the time and that he didn't regret his actions.

His defence was insanity and any absence of motive, but the jury took just four minutes to reach their verdict and Cudworth was duly convicted of wilful murder.

17

ON HER BIRTHDAY

Edward Hemmings, 4 April 1893

Twenty-six-year-old collier Ted Hemmings had married Annie Haigh at Whitsuntide 1892. At five years his junior, gregarious and attractive Annie was very different in character from the staid and morose Hemmings, and even his close friends and family were surprised that she had accepted his offer of marriage.

Any happiness Annie may have felt following her wedding was soon shattered when she discovered her husband was heavily in debt. Following a number of visits from bailiffs and creditors, the couple had to flee their home in Normanton and moved to Sheffield, taking lodgings in the suburb of Woodhouse.

Hemmings soon found a job in the mines and the couple began to furnish their new home with items of furniture bought on hire purchase. However, they soon began to quarrel and as a result Hemmings moved out of the house on Robins Lane, leaving Annie alone in the home. Although she quickly found a variety of jobs bringing her a small income, she soon fell behind with the hire purchase repayments and the furniture was repossessed.

Throughout the separation, Hemmings had maintained to friends that he was in love with Annie, and early in 1893 he persuaded her to give their marriage another try and they moved into new lodgings across the town. No sooner had they moved into their rooms than Hemmings reverted back to his old ways. He became jealous of her talking to other lodgers in the communal kitchen at their lodgings, and despite her pleas for him to save money so they could find better housing, he seemed content to stay off work for the slightest excuse.

Friday 17 February 1893 was Annie's 22nd birthday. On the previous evening they stayed in their room and seemed cheerful enough when their landlady popped in to bid them goodnight.

Edward Hemmings was convicted of the murder of his wife. (T.J. Leech Archive)

But in the early hours of Friday morning, one of the lodgers was woken by sounds of a disturbance coming from the Hemmings' room. He called out and asked if everything was all right. Hemmings replied there was nothing wrong and he was heard leaving the house at 4 a.m., the usual time when he was on the early shift at work.

Later that morning the lodger knocked on the door to check on Annie. He called out and, receiving no reply, he opened the door and recoiled in horror. Annie Hemmings was lying on the bedroom floor with a huge gash in her neck, and cuts to her forehead. Bloodstains covered the wall.

The police were called and, once a surgeon had confirmed that there was no way the wounds could have been self-inflicted, a murder hunt began. Hemmings had not gone into work and it was found that he had subsequently gone to Doncaster before making his way to Normanton, where he confessed to police.

Hemmings found himself before Mr Justice Bruce at Leeds Assizes on 15 March. It was a straightforward case; Hemmings was jealous of the friendship between wife and other lodgers and in a jealous rage he had killed her with an axe, which he had discarded as he left the house. Police had discovered the bloodstained weapon under a railway arch and it was identified as belonging to the killer. Following conviction, he left a full confession.

18

FOR THAT PURPOSE

Philip Garner, 3 April 1894

It was while serving as a mess sergeant in Belfast that Philip Garner met his wife to be. Following their marriage, Philip and Agnes Garner returned to England and initially set up home in Liverpool, where Garner found work as a labourer at the docks. However, by the autumn of 1893, 49-year-old Garner and his 44-year-old wife had been parted for over two years, and during that time both had settled in Yorkshire; she at Doncaster while he lived a short distance further north, near Askern.

On Saturday 25 November, Garner sought out his wife and she agreed with his request to spend the night together. They took lodgings in Doncaster with a man named Richard Hoyle, and after spending the evening drinking they returned to their lodgings. Hoyle saw them as they returned home and they seemed happy together.

On the following lunchtime they had gone out for a meal and a few drinks, after which they were seen walking together in the direction of a field in an area known locally as Low Pastures. A short time later, two young boys saw Garner walking away from the field rubbing his hands on his clothes. He then walked to the nearest police station and asked the desk sergeant if Low Pastures was in his jurisdiction. Told it was, he confessed that he had killed his wife and made a detailed statement:

> I have killed my wife with a hammer… I knocked her skull in. Look, there is blood on my hands. You'll find her in a ditch by the stone style. The hammer is by her side… I tried to do it before but failed.

Agnes Garner was found alive, but died from her injuries a few days later and Garner was then arraigned to stand trial for murder at Leeds Assizes, which were due to sit just a matter of days later. It was then decided to postpone the trial pending a medical enquiry and he was removed to Wakefield Gaol, where he was kept under observation with regards to his mental state.

On Tuesday 13 March 1894, Garner appeared before Mr Justice Collins at Leeds Assizes. The prosecution pointed to a statement Garner had made following his arrest, in which he claimed that he had killed her because she had left him and had taken up with another man. 'I could not take it anymore,' he said, adding, 'so I decided to kill her and took her to the field for that purpose.'

His defence of insanity was rejected, he was sentenced to death and became the second of three people hanged in three days by James Billington, who had travelled to Leeds having hanged a woman in Liverpool on the previous day, Easter Monday, and who had an engagement in Birmingham the following morning.

19

'FOR A DEED I NEVER DONE'

Alfred Dews, 21 August 1894

Alfred Dews believed that his newborn son was another man's child. He suspected his wife had been unfaithful and although she did all she could to placate him; he refused to listen and showed no affection to the boy they named Benjamin.

Dews and his wife had married in 1890 and she soon bore him a son, Herbert. The family lived at Swales Buildings, New Scarborough, Wakefield, where Dews earned a living as an iron-moulder. Shortly after the birth of their second child, in the spring of 1894, Dews procured from a workmate a bottle of 'sal volatile' and ammonia carbonate, used as smelling salts. He told the man he was suffering from fainting and headaches and he had heard it would help his problems.

On Saturday 12 May, Dews and his wife were home, along with a 12-year-old neighbour, Eliza Hobson, who was helping to look after the child. After lunch Mrs Dews announced that she needed to run an errand and left her husband and the young girl alone with the baby.

No sooner had his wife left than Dews asked Eliza if she would go fetch him a gill of beer from the local off-licence. She did as she was asked and when she returned five minutes later she could see that something was amiss.

'What's the matter with the baby?' she cried, seeing the young child screaming and vomiting. A neighbour was alerted by her cries and saw that the child's mouth was a vivid red colour and its breath smelt strange. She asked Dews if he would call a doctor but he flatly refused. Mrs Dews soon returned, by which time the neighbour had voiced her concerns to another neighbour who in turn had alerted the police.

An officer arrived at the house and while the child was removed to the local infirmary, the house was searched and the bottle of smelling salts was discovered. Four days later, police asked a chemical analyst from Sheffield to examine the child and the smelling salts. Although he was able to confirm that it appeared the child had ingested an irritant consistent with the bottle he tested, which had blistered inside his mouth, the passage of time from the suspected poisoning meant that any traces of poison had now passed from the child's body.

Ten days later the baby died, and Dews was charged with murder by poisoning and arraigned to stand trial at the next assizes. In July Dews found himself before Mr Justice Grantham, and although he maintained from the moment of the child being taken ill until he stood in the dock that he was innocent, the prosecution produced witnesses who suggested there was a motive for the crime.

A neighbour testified that shortly after the birth of his son, Dews swore at his wife and accused her of being unfaithful. He had also kicked and punched her, despite her pleas for him to believe her and stop the attack. It took the jury just fifteen minutes to reach their verdict, although they did ask the judge to recommend mercy.

Alfred Dews maintained his innocence to the end, and when his wife visited him on the eve of his execution he handed her a will telling her how to dispose of his property. There was little sympathy for the poisoner locally, although his wife told a newspaper after her farewell interview that she would gladly forgive him if his life could be spared.

20

'EVEN IF I HAVE TO LOSE MY LIFE FOR IT!'

Patrick Morley, 31 December 1895

In the summer of 1894, Irish labourer Patrick Morley lived with his wife Elizabeth on Hunslet Lane, Leeds. In July of that year she took out a summons against him when he pointed a gun at her and made threats against her. A year later they had moved to Batley and, tired of his constant violence towards her, Elizabeth again had cause to report him when he made further threats against her. Morley was bound over to keep the peace for six months, but by early September his behaviour was such that Elizabeth fled their lodging and moved to another house across town.

On 14 September the Batley Feast opened and 38-year-old Morley sought out and met up with his wife for the first time in more than a week. He asked her to take him back but she refused. He continued to ask her to take him back every day for the next week and she repeatedly refused, telling him on one day, 'even if I have to lose my life for it!'

On 22 September Morley called again on his wife and asked her to lend him a shilling. She refused, saying that as she had been off work she had not made any money. They began to quarrel, during which he pulled out his revolver and shot her. He then turned the gun on himself, but was trembling so much that he missed when he pulled the trigger and he was quickly overpowered and placed under arrest.

Tried before Mr Justice Grantham in December, Morley claimed that the gun had gone off accidentally. Statements Morley had made following his arrest showed that he had been jealous of his wife and angry that she would not take him back. The prosecution used this to show that rather than an accident, the murder had been premeditated because Elizabeth refused to take him back.

21

LIKE AN INFURIATED ANIMAL

Joseph Robert Ellis, 25 August 1896

Twenty-two-year-old former sailor Joe Ellis and his wife, Emma, also 22, had lived in Back South Street, Goole, since their wedding in the previous spring, when in June 1896, tired of his cruelty, they parted. Emma went back to live with her mother, complaining that her husband favoured the company of other women, often lost his temper, and acted on occasions 'like an infuriated animal.' It was a foretaste of things to come.

At teatime on Wednesday 1 July, Ellis called at his mother-in-law's house and asked Emma to sign some forms regarding their house. She put her signature on a document and, as she passed it back to Ellis, she made some remark causing him to push past her, and pulling out a knife he slashed out at his wife's mother, Sarah Woomock, cutting her in the head. He then turned on his wife and cut her on the neck.

Both women fled the house screaming, and made for the shelter of a neighbour's home. Moments later, Ellis kicked open the door and burst inside as the terrified women fled out of the back door. Ellis caught up with them in the backyard, where he stabbed his wife in the breast and bowel, causing her dreadful injuries.

Realising what he had done, Ellis went back into the front street, where he attempted to sharpen his knife on a kerbstone before pulling the knife across his own throat, causing just a minor wound. He then put down the knife and walked across to the nearby Mariner's Arms public house, where he ordered a glass of beer. He was arrested as he finished his drink and taken into custody. Emma Ellis and her mother were both taken to hospital, where Emma's condition deteriorated during the night. She was able to make a statement before she slumped into unconsciousness. She died from her wounds in the early hours.

Ellis stood trial before Mr Justice Kennedy at Leeds on Monday 3 August. His defence was based on provocation and that the prisoner was insane at the time of the murder. The prosecution claimed that it was an unprovoked and vicious

Newscutting describing the Goole Murder. (T.J. Leech Archive)

assault by a man who had been described in the past as acting like an infuriated animal, and who had shown those same characteristics again when he committed a brutal murder. The jury agreed and took just twenty minutes to reach their verdict of guilty as charged.

22

'A GUN AND SIX PENNETH OF LAUDANUM'

Joseph Robinson, 17 August 1897

Joseph Robinson, a 33-year-old miner of Worsborough Bridge, on the outskirts of Barnsley, had been married to his 24-year-old wife Florence for eight years when she finally left him. They had frequently quarrelled during their marriage, and she had walked out on a number of occasions, but it was after she was forced to take out a summons for aggravated assault against him that she decided enough was enough.

Taking their young daughter, Florence fled the area and went to stay with her sister at nearby Monk Bretton, and for most of the spring of 1897 managed to keep away from her husband.

On Tuesday 11 May, Robinson discovered his wife's whereabouts and on the following morning he went shopping, purchasing, as he would state later, 'a gun and six penneth of laudanum.' At noon that day he approached the house at Monk Bretton. He knocked on the door and when his wife saw who the caller was she ran through the house and tried to flee through the back door. Robinson fired a shot, which missed and embedded itself in the doorframe; the second struck his wife in the head, just below the ear, blowing away her jaw and killing her instantly. As his wife slumped to the ground Robinson gulped down the laudanum.

Police were quickly at the scene and Robinson was rushed to Barnsley's Beckett Hospital, where prompt medical treatment prevented him from cheating justice. He was convicted on overwhelming evidence before Mr Justice Wright at Leeds Assizes on Thursday 29 July, and on the gallows he said he was sorry for the pain he had caused his little daughter.

23

A GESTURE OF GOOD WILL

Walter Robinson, 17 August 1897

It was a gesture of goodwill that was to cost Sarah Pickles her life. Forty-year-old Sarah lived in the village of Thornton, on the outskirts of Bradford, and had come to the aid of her cousin, 33-year-old

Walter Robinson, a former soldier, policeman and tram driver, when, following a quarrel with his landlady, he was thrown onto the streets. She was soon to regret making the offer. Robinson, now working as a wool comber, was a heavy drinker and his drunken behaviour soon gave her cause for concern. She tried to warn him about his drinking and bad language in the house and when he took no heed of her words she resorted to taking legal action and he was subsequently bound over to keep the peace, and told to find fresh lodgings.

Robinson was incensed, and although he soon found alternative accommodation, on Friday evening, 11 June 1897, while out drinking, he began to make threats that he would 'do for Sarah before the weekend was out!'

Later that night he returned to Sarah's house, barged his way in and locked the door. He then pulled out his razor and began a fearsome attack, slashing her face and neck over a dozen times before hacking at her stricken body as it lay lifeless on the ground. Her screams had brought the neighbouring elderly couple to the window to see what was happening, and when Robinson noticed their presence he dragged them inside, locked the door and fled.

However, they soon managed to flee the house and alert the police, who arrested Robinson at his new lodgings. After committing the murder he had walked across to a nearby stream and washed his hands, razor and the blood from his clothes, and when he returned home he hung the wet clothes beside the fire and retired to bed.

Following his arrest, Robinson told officers that he blamed drink for the crime, but added, 'I am satisfied, I have got my revenge.'

Robinson was convicted before Mr Justice Wright at Leeds Assizes at the end of July after his plea of insanity failed. As he awaited execution, he became so distraught at his impending doom that the prison authorities feared he would try to pre-empt the sentence and posted extra warders in his cell to prevent any suicide attempts.

24

'BIG ENOUGH TO HOLD THEM AND ME AND ALL'

Thomas Mellor, 16 August 1900

On 5 May 1900, 29-year-old Thomas Mellor, a gasworks labourer from Holbeck, Leeds, paid a visit to his brother. On the previous day, Mellor, along with his girlfriend and his two daughters, 6-year-old Ada and 4-year-old Annie Beechcroft, had been told that children were not welcome at the lodging house and had to find a new place to live.

The young girls were Mellor's step-daughters; their mother, Ada Beecroft, had been committed to an asylum shortly after the birth of Annie, where she died in November 1899. With his wife in the asylum, Mellor had began a relationship with a woman named Priscilla Redshaw, and she had helped Mellor look after the children after his wife died.

The Mellor family had been living in squalor and it was in desperation that he had asked his brother, Arthur, if they could stay with him until they found new lodgings that accepted children. Arthur Mellor reluctantly told him there was not enough room, while his wife was concerned enough to ask Mellor what he planned to do, as she was aware he had failed in an earlier attempt to have them housed in a workhouse. Whether it was a threat or just a throwaway remark, Mellor said that unless they found new lodgings soon he would do something desperate. 'The water is big enough to hold them and me and all,' he told her.

At around 9.30 p.m. on Saturday 11 May, Mellor and his daughters left the house, telling Priscilla they would be back the following morning. Witnesses later saw a man and two young girls walking along the pathway of the Leeds/Liverpool canal, and at 11.30 p.m. a man matching Mellor's description was seen alone. The following morning the bodies of the two girls were found floating in the canal close to Globe Road, Holbeck.

Mellor was soon arrested and at his trial before Mr Justice Ridley at the end of July he confessed to putting the girls into the canal, but that he had not intended to drown them. Although charged with the murder of both girls, he was tried for just the murder of his daughter, Ada. His defence was that he had been on the canal bank when he saw two men approaching. Mellor said that he decided to put the children into what he believed was a shallow part of the water then flee, and that their cries would attract the attention of the passers-by who would then hopefully look after the children.

Mellor's counsel also claimed at the trial that he had been driven to abandon the children by the Holbeck Board of State who had refused him aid in looking after the children, although when he had been arrested Mellor was in possession of enough money to afford lodgings for his family.

The prosecution claimed it was a brutal murder committed by a man who wanted to be free from the burden of the two young girls. In summing up the judge sided with the prosecution, and said that if Mellor's intention was to leave the girls to be found by passers-by, then clearly it would have made sense to merely leave the children on the streets, where a policeman could have taken them in safely. Surprisingly, following the reaching of a guilty verdict, the jury added a strong recommendation to mercy, due to his previous kindness to his children.

25

THE FIRST BULLET

Charles Benjamin Backhouse, 16 August 1900

On 5 July 1900, a summons was issued against 19-year-old Fred Backhouse for an assault he had made on his 23-year-old brother Charlie's wife. Fred lodged at the house and the summons was served by PC John William Kew, who was stationed at Rotherham. The Backhouse family were well known to the police; with a reputation for violence, and officers were frequent visitors to the house at 75 Piccadilly, in the Swinton district of Rotherham.

The summons was due to be answered on 9 July, but two days before the brothers vanished from the area, and when Fred Backhouse failed to appear, the court in his absence fined him 40s or one month's prison sentence.

A few days later, Charlie purchased a revolver and nine cartridges, and later that night the brothers were out drinking when Charlie pulled out the gun and began making threats to drinkers and passers-by. The following day, Tuesday 10 July, PC Kew was detailed to follow up the complaint and went to investigate the allegations.

> **Chief Constable's Office,**
> WAKEFIELD, JULY 28TH, 1900.
>
> ### Circular Memo.
>
> ## Late Police Constable No. 680 John Wm. Kew.
>
> The Chief Constable deeply regrets having to announce to the Force that at 11.30 p.m. on the 10th instant, POLICE CONSTABLE No. 680 JOHN WILLIAM KEW, of the West Riding Constabulary, stationed at Swinton, near Rotherham, was murdered upon the Highway by being shot with a revolver by Charles Benjamin Backhouse and Frederick Lawder Backhouse.
>
> The late P.C. Kew had creditably served in this Force for over five years, and has left a widow and four small children entirely unprovided for.
>
> The Chief Constable is sure that he has only to make this sad and lamentable circumstance generally known to ensure from every member of the Force such a gratuitous and charitable response to an appeal for aid to the bereaved widow and children, in this their time of severe affliction and pressing need, as may in some degree tend, temporarily as well as permanently, to relieve their sudden and unexpected distress.
>
> Superintendents will, therefore, on next pay-day, ascertain the feelings of the men of their respective Divisions on this subject, and any subscriptions which they may be disposed to give for the benefit of the widow and children will be forwarded, with the names of the subscribers, to this Office.
>
> A List of the Subscriptions will afterwards be published.
>
> BY ORDER,
> **WM. SMITH GILL,**
> D. C. C. & CHIEF CLERK.
>
> THE SUPERINTENDENTS,
> West Riding Constabulary.

An appeal by the Chief Constable for financial help from officers following the murder of PC Kew.

PC Kew arrived at Piccadilly just as the brothers were leaving for work. He told them he had heard reports they were carrying a firearm and asked to search them. He moved towards Charlie Backhouse, who took a step backward, whipped out the gun and fired once, striking Kew in the stomach. The constable slumped forward but managed to grab the older brother by the hands and point the gun away. As they grappled on the floor, Fred Backhouse pulled the gun from his brother's hand and pointed it at PC Kew.

'Here's another for you,' he shouted, firing another shot into Kew's side.

The brothers fled as Kew collapsed, before being assisted into his own home close by. He was able to make a statement naming his attackers before he lapsed into unconsciousness. He died the following day, the post-mortem showing that the first bullet had proved fatal.

The brothers were soon under arrest and less than a month later they stood trial before Mr Justice Ridley at Leeds Assizes. Fred admitted his guilt but claimed he was drunk at the time. In reaching their verdict, the jury believed Charles Backhouse was guilty as charged, but in the case of his younger brother they asked if they could return a verdict of aiding and abetting.

The judge explained that as the two men were present when the murder took place, and that both had fired at the officer, even though it was Charles who had fired the first and fatal bullet, by aiding and abetting in the crime Fred was still just as guilty of murder.

As they announced their verdict of guilt in both cases, the foreman said that in respect of Fred Backhouse they recommended him to mercy on account of his age. Both were sentenced to death and scheduled to hang alongside child-killer Thomas Mellor (*see* Chapter 24), convicted at the same assizes. There hadn't been a triple execution carried out anywhere in the country since 1896, but procedures were put into place should it go ahead.

As it turned out, Fred Backhouse was granted a reprieve two days before he was due to hang. There was no such mercy for Charlie Backhouse or Thomas Mellor and they were hanged side by side.

PC John Kew, shot dead by the Backhouse brothers. (T.J. Leech Archive)

26

THE BEESTON TRAGEDY

Charles Oliver Blewitt, 28 August 1900

The curtains of the house at 7 Star Fold, Beeston, Leeds, had remained closed for the last week. There were no comings and goings, nor was there any signs of the tenants, Charlie Blewitt, a 33-year-old tanner, and his wife of the same age, Mary Ann. They had last been seen over a week before, and so, on 17 June 1900, worried relatives of both Blewitt and his wife got in touch with the landlord and asked to be let into the house to see if there were any clues to their disappearance.

Opening the door they were greeted with a dreadful smell that acted as warning of what they were to find. In the living room, sitting in a rocking chair, a shawl covering her head, was the body of Mary Ann Blewitt. Her throat had been cut and there were cuts to her arms and hands. Beside the body was a dried pool of blood, which contained a distinctive boot print. A post-mortem found that Mary Blewitt had been dead for at least seven days before she was discovered.

The missing husband became the prime suspect. Blewitt had been unemployed for several weeks and relations between husband and wife had suffered since he had lost his job. As the murder enquiry took place in Leeds, Blewitt was in Halifax, where, under the alias Oliver Jackson, he found a job, and where, on 3 July, he was arrested.

Blewitt claimed he had travelled to Halifax to find work and that his wife had been alive when he left her. He even suggested that if she was dead then she must have taken her own life. Blewitt's boots were examined and besides having a similar pattern to the one found at the scene of the murder, there were also traces of blood on them.

His first trial took place at Leeds Assizes before Mr Justice Ridley at the same sittings as the Backhouse and Mellor cases. The defence maintained that Blewitt was innocent and asked what motive there was for him to kill his wife. They maintained that Mary Ann Blewitt must have committed suicide, although a police surgeon said that there were wounds on the hands and arms that had most likely been caused as she fought off an attacker.

Despite this, it seemed that the defence were able to put enough doubt into the minds of the jury that they failed to reach a verdict. A week later, before a new trial judge, the prosecution's case again failed to show a realistic motive, although much was made of the bloodstained footprints, which matched those of Blewitt's. This time the jury found the prisoner guilty as charged and it was left for Mr Justice Bruce to pass sentence in the usual manner.

27

'THE NATURAL AVENGER AND PROTECTOR'

John Gallagher & Emily Swann, 29 December 1903

William and Emily Swann lived at George Square, at Wombwell, Barnsley. They had been married for over twenty years and had raised eleven children, when some time in 1902 they took a lodger, a 30-year-old miner named John Gallagher. Within a short time Gallagher, a former soldier, began an affair with his 42-year-old landlady. Her husband, a 44-year-old glass blower, soon became suspicious of goings on at the house while he worked the nightshift, and early in 1903 he ordered Gallagher to leave.

Over the next few weeks, Gallagher paid regular visits back to George Square, with each visit ending with threats and fights between the two men. Gallagher then took lodgings with a Mrs Lavinia Ward, who lived directly opposite the Swann's house on George's Square. On Saturday 6 June, Gallagher and Mrs Swann spent the afternoon drinking with other tenants at his lodgings, and when Mrs Swann returned home later that evening she received a beating from her husband.

'See what our Bill has done,' she told Gallagher, who replied that he would, 'Go and give him something for himself – I will kick his ribs in!'

Gallagher then left the house, followed by Mrs Swann and other tenants, to one of whom Mrs Swann said, 'I hope he punches him to death, and I hope he kills the bastard.' Gallagher burst into Swann's house as Mrs Swann shouted, 'Give it to the bastard, Johnny.'

A fight ensued, and when Gallagher returned to his lodgings ten minutes later he boasted that he had broken four of William's ribs and would break four more. Gallagher and Mrs Swann then returned to the house, where a further struggle took place. Ten minutes later the couple stood hand-in-hand at

John Gallagher and Emily Swan in the dock at the trial for the murder of her husband. (T.J. Leech Archive)

the door, before Gallagher left to return home. A few minutes later, Mrs Swann asked a neighbour to check on her husband who found William Swann lying dead in the back kitchen, his head propped up against a cupboard. Lying beside the body was a bloodstained poker.

When police arrived at George Street, Gallagher had fled, but Mrs Swann was taken into custody and held on remand as a manhunt was launched. For two months Gallagher tramped around North Yorkshire, pawning his clothing to obtain money for food, until on 4 August, half starved and 'out on his feet', he turned up in his native Middlesbrough, where he was arrested at his sister's home.

Mr Justice Darling presided over events when Gallagher and Mrs Swann stood trial together at West Riding Assizes on Wednesday 9 December. The prosecution alleged it was a brutal murder committed as a punishment for the black eye Swann had given to his wife following her infidelity. Defence counsel Mr Mitchell Innes vainly tried to show that Gallagher had gone to the house merely to admonish to the husband chastisement for the brutal beating of his wife. He also explained that the 'murder' had not been premeditated and had been inflamed by passion, excitement and drink. 'Gallagher,' Innes said, had merely overdone his role as 'the natural avenger and protector.' At no time did he intend to commit murder.

Summing up, Mr Justice Darling told the jury that if it could be found that the killing had been committed under great provocation then there may be reasonable grounds for a verdict of manslaughter. He also pointed to the evidence that Mrs Swann had taken an active part in the killing, not by her immediate actions but by her verbal encouragements, as had been testified by a number of witnesses. The jury needed just forty minutes to find both the accused guilty as charged.

Asked if they had anything to say before sentence of death was passed, Gallagher declined, but Mrs Swann rose to her feet and declared, 'Yes, I am innocent! I am not afraid of immediate death because I am innocent and will go to God!' Until the very end Mrs Swann believed she would be reprieved, but when word reached the prison on the day before she was to be hanged that the Home Secretary had declined mercy, she collapsed in a fit of hysteria. Gallagher, having stoically accepted his fate, told his guards that he never expected a reprieve.

Assistant hangman Ellis described Mrs Swann as a little, stumpy, round-faced woman, standing a little less than 5ft tall and weighing just 122lb. They had been kept apart since conviction, their only meeting being at a short service in the prison chapel on Christmas Day. There next meeting was when the stood side by side on the scaffold. When hangman John Billington, officiating at just his second execution, entered the condemned cell, Mrs Swann was lying in a prostrate heap on her cell floor overcome with terror. By the time she was assisted to the scaffold she had regained enough composure to speak to her lover for the last time.

'Good morning, John,' she said to her hooded companion.

'Good morning, love,' he replied, as the hangman placed the rope around her neck.

'Goodbye love, God bless you,' she whispered, as Billington darted to the lever and sprung the trap.

28

A TRAIL OF BLOOD

James Henry Clarkson, 29 March 1904

Sitting in his cell at Armley Gaol, the young man counted down the days to his execution, frequently bursting into tears and crying over and over, 'What made me do it?' That had been the question debated before Mr Justice Lawrence at York Assizes in March 1904, when James Clarkson stood in the dock accused of a quite brutal murder.

Twelve-year-old Elizabeth Mary Lynas was last seen alive by friends as she walked home from church on Sunday evening, 27 December 1903. Reaching the corner of Bennison Street, Guisborough, Cleveland, Elizabeth said goodnight to her friends and set off towards her home at No. 17. She never arrived.

Later that night her worried parents went to the police station and reported her as missing. A search was made of the streets and the nearby woods, and in the early hours her body was discovered close to the local workhouse. She had been savagely assaulted: her wrists and ankles

The Illustrated Police News *reports the murder of Elizabeth Lynas. (T.J. Leech Archive)*

were tied with a clothesline and her throat cut from ear to ear. There were other marks of violence on the body, but although her clothing was ripped and torn she had not been sexually assaulted. It was assumed the killer had been disturbed and had fled before he could sate his wicked lust.

Suspicion fell on Clarkson, a 19-year-old tailor who lived five houses away with his sister and father, when a trail of blood led police to his back yard. The house was searched and hidden in a kitchen cupboard was a bloodstained razor. In Clarkson's bedroom was a bloodstained towel and clothes with traces of blood. Clarkson claimed that he had been in a public house until 8.20 p.m., but nobody was able to substantiate his alibi.

Throughout the trial, Clarkson steadfastly maintained his innocence, though the evidence gathered from his house, circumstantial though it may have been, was enough to convince the jury he was indeed the killer and they needed just thirty minutes to reach their verdict. Although he was recommended to mercy on account of his youth, no reprieve was forthcoming and he was hanged just two days before his twentieth birthday.

James Henry Clarkson was hanged two days before his 20th birthday. (T.J. Leech Archive)

29

HER OTHER MEN

John Thomas Kay, 16 August 1904

It was a startling revelation. Approaching a police officer, 52-year-old John Kay asked the constable for directions to the local police station and, once pointed in the right direction, he took a deep breath and blurted out, 'I might as well tell you, it's murder I think. I've killed the woman I live with. I did it with a hatchet.' Kay went on to say that he had hit the woman at least three or four times, he was not sure exactly how many. It was Tuesday afternoon, 10 May 1904.

Kay lived with his paramour on Sheffield Road, in the Ickles area of Rotherham, and when officers called at the house they found 28-year-old Jane Hirst unconscious but still alive. She had a number of severe head wounds, and although a doctor was summoned she died before she could be taken to hospital. Jane Hirst had been living with Kay since September 1903. She was a married woman but had separated from her husband following numerous quarrels about her drinking, and, moving in with Kay, they had a tempestuous relationship, which often resulted in violence. On one occasion in April they had had a quarrel that resulted in Jane being thrown out and with Kay refusing to let her back in until the following day, when she had sobered up.

Kay was tried at Leeds Assizes before Mr Justice Channell in July, and his defence was that he was under the influence of drink at the time of the attack. Kay claimed that they had been drinking constantly for many weeks, in her case because she was an alcoholic, while in his case because he had learned of her other men.

Kay said he had recently discovered that Jane had been unfaithful to him and it had preyed upon his mind. He had already made one attempt at suicide because of this knowledge and it was while in a rage he had battered her to death.

His defence claimed that Kay was insane, that he had heard voices urging him to kill and that he was suffering from what was termed 'impulsive insanity'. All this, they alleged, showed a clear indication that his mind was unhinged at the time of the murder and that the charge should be one of guilty of manslaughter. The jury disagreed, and John Kay was hanged on 16 August 1904.

Newspaper sketch of John Kay. (T.J. Leech Archive)

30

THE SON-IN-LAW

Edmund Hall, 20 December 1904

'I was a soldier once. Now I am soldier of Jesus Christ.'

The last words of Edmund Hall, December 1904

At 78 years of age, widower John Dalby shared his home at 4 Alma Terrace, off Fulford Road, York, with his daughter and son-in-law, Mr and Mrs Francis Chatwin. During the day the Chatwins ran a shop on Newgate, leaving the old man alone in the house. At lunchtime on 29 July 1904 a man approached the house and shortly after he was seen entering, neighbours heard sounds of a struggle, followed by moaning. They went to investigate and receiving no answer at the front door, they approached the back where the door was slowly opened by the old man, who staggered and fell into their arms. Bleeding profusely from wound to the neck, Dalby tried to speak but was unable to utter a word.

'Fetch the doctor,' called one of the neighbours, and at that moment a man came tearing out of the house, leapt over the back wall, and disappeared down the street. A doctor was soon at the scene, but Dalby died in hospital a short time later.

As Dalby was being taken to hospital, detectives arrived at Alma Terrace, where one of the neighbours told them the identity of the attacker. She gave his name as Dalby's son-in-law Edmund Hall. Forty-nine-year-old former soldier, Hall worked as a labourer and lived with his wife, Dalby's daughter, in Leeds. With Hall known to have come from Leeds, it was just a simple matter to work out that he had probably travelled to the city by train, and would more than likely try to return home the same way. No trains had left since the crime was reported and officers were posted to watch for passengers boarding Leeds-bound trains.

Sure enough, later that night Hall was seen entering a carriage at the station and was smoking a cigar waiting for its departure when detectives approached him. While being questioned at the local police station, Hall was noticed to be wearing a gold watch and chain, identified as being one Dalby was known to wear, and which his daughter confirmed he had been wearing earlier in the day.

Edmund Hall, murdered his father-in-law at York. (T.J. Leech Archive)

Hall was tried before Mr Justice Darling, on Thursday 1 December. The prosecution claimed that Hall was guilty of a most atrocious murder, carried out in the furtherance of theft.

The defence attempted to show that the prisoner was insane. The court heard that Hall had served with the army in India and had been discharged in 1879, suffering from sunstroke-induced melancholia. On his return to England he had then been injured in a lift accident, which had also affected his mind. Remanded pending trial, he was held at Wakefield Gaol, where the medical officer testified that he had examined Hall a length and was of the opinion that even the smallest of causes could provoke him to violence.

The prosecution countered this by showing that on the day before he committed the murder Hall had tried unsuccessfully to buy a gun and, failing this, he had travelled to York carrying a razor. The purpose of the visit was to commit a robbery; he knew the old man would be in the house alone, and he knew that his brother-in-law kept money from the shop's profits in a safe at Alma Terrace, which he intended to steal.

31

THE POACHERS

Arthur Jeffries, 28 December 1904

Arthur Jeffries, a 44-year-old cobbler, was one of a gang of poachers who worked in and around Rotherham. Among the gang was Jeffries' best friend, Samuel Barker, but in October 1904 they fell

Poacher Arthur Jeffries. (T.J. Leech Archive)

out when Barker and the rest of the gang went out poaching one night without him. Jeffries seethed and issued threats against the gang that he would 'do for' one of them.

Late on the night of 12 November, four of the poachers, including Barker, were walking home together when they met up with Arthur Jeffries as they passed close by his home. Walking past Jeffries, who was stood at the end of his street, Barker bid his friend goodnight.

'Good night to you too, you bugger,' Jeffries answered.

Barker laughed and retorted, 'Well bugger you too, Arthur.'

What had been a harmless remark took on grave consequences. Jeffries struck out at Barker and the fight spilled into an adjacent alley where Barker fell to the ground, a deep stab wound in his side. Carried to a friend's house, he died within minutes.

Following his arrest, Jeffries expressed genuine remorse over what he had done, although the murder weapon, believed to be a heavy engineer's file, was never discovered. Jeffries was tried before Mr Justice Grantham at Leeds Assizes on 8 December. The judge, a country squire, was known to have little sympathy for people involved in poaching, as his own land was often the subject to poaching.

The defence sought to show that there was no premeditation in the attack, that before the murder both men had been the best of friends, and as the fatal blow had been struck in the heat of the moment, during a fight, therefore his crime was one of manslaughter.

The judge came down on the side of the prosecution and directed the jury that if they believed that Jeffries had killed Barker, then the only possible verdict was murder. The jury took just over thirty minutes to return a guilty verdict, adding a strong recommendation for mercy, but he was sentenced to death.

32

'IF YOU SCREAM, I WILL KILL YOU'

Thomas George Tattersall, 15 August 1905

Thomas Tattersall was no stranger to the inside of an execution chamber. In the spring of 1905, the 31-year-old plasterer had been employed at Wakefield Gaol, detailed to work on the new execution chamber being constructed.

Tattersall lived with his wife Rebecca and their four children at Wakefield. They did not live happily together and often quarrelled, which over the months became more frequent and much more violent. As a result, Rebecca had appealed to her brother for protection and when he was unable to help she contacted the police, who placed the house under supervision, with officers making regular visits to check all was well.

Despite the visits from the police, early in June Tattersall assaulted his wife and tried to strangle her, and a few weeks later he assaulted her again and threatened to kill her. In the early hours of Monday 3 July, their 10-year-old daughter heard some strange gurgling noises coming from her parents' bedroom. As she went to investigate she came across her father heading downstairs.

'If you scream, I will kill you,' Tattersall told the terrified child as he headed for the door. When she entered her parents' bedroom she found her mother lying in bed, her throat cut and head battered with a hatchet.

Tattersall was soon arrested and confessed that he attacked his wife with a hatchet, then cut her throat, but had no idea he was doing wrong.

At his trial at Leeds Assizes, before Mr Justice Jelf, Tattersall's counsel claimed that he was suicidal, was suffering from homicidal mania, and that he was not responsible for his actions. Tattersall was duly convicted of murder and executed at Leeds just six weeks after murdering his wife. His execution also happened to be the last for the hangman, John Billington.

Billington fell through an open trapdoor while preparing the drop, and although he was able to carry out the execution on the following morning, he died a few weeks later as a result of internal injuries sustained in the accident.

John Billington. The hangman suffered an unfortunate injury while preparing the gallows for Tattersall's execution. (Author's Collection)

33

THE ILKLEY MURDER

George Smith, 28 December 1905

In the summer of 1905, Martha Smith found a position as a domestic worker for Harold Shelton, in Burley Road, Leeds. She had not been in the post long when Shelton came home to find her hiding in the kitchen, her lip split and face bruised. She told him that her husband had called at the house, they had argued and he had struck her.

The Illustrated Police News *records the murder of Martha Smith. (T.J. Leech Archive)*

Her husband was George Smith, a 50-year-old bricklayer, and when he made a further visit to the house, Shelton chastised him for hitting a woman and told him not to call again. Although remorseful at first, Smith returned the following day and demanded that Martha hand in her notice, and after a long argument, during which threats were made, Martha reluctantly agreed.

She initially went to stay at her mother's house at Wakefield, but soon took another position, this time with the Glendenning family who lived at the Kells, on Riddings Road, Ilkley. At 6.30 p.m. on 12 September, the Glendenning's teenage daughter arrived home and was surprised to find the back door locked. She called out and, getting no reply, she managed to gain entry through the cellar kitchen, where she stumbled across the body of Martha Smith lying in a pool of blood.

Martha's throat had been cut and she had over forty stab wounds to her body. The police had only one suspect and Smith was arrested in Wakefield two days later. Questioned by detectives, Smith said that he gone to Ilkley to speak to his wife. She had then told him the marriage was over and she had found herself another man. They began to quarrel and during the struggle Smith pulled out his knife and stabbed her repeatedly.

His trial before Mr Justice Jelf on 7 December was a formality. The defence was based on provocation, as Smith claimed that his wife had attacked him first. Smith also claimed he had no recollection of cutting his wife's throat, but the prosecution built up a strong case and showed that on the day of the murder he had told his landlady he was going to look for work in Halifax, but when he left she noticed that a knife was missing. This implied that Smith intended to kill his wife, as he had taken the knife for a purpose.

It took the jury an hour to return their verdict, and there were loud cheers from the public gallery as sentence of death was passed.

34

'JUST A BIT OF BOTHER'

John William Ellwood, 3 December 1908

It was Friday 31 July 1908, when a man passing the offices of the Fieldhouse and Jowett dye works in Bradford thought he heard sounds of moaning coming from inside the building. He spied through a window and noticed a figure lying on the floor, covered in blood. Alerting the police, it was soon established the man was Thomas Wilkinson, who worked in the factory as a cashier, and that he had been the victim of a savage beating. Wilkinson was taken to hospital but was too badly injured to save, and he passed away shortly after.

A bloodstained poker was found beside the body and a large amount of cash was missing from the safe. When police started appealing for information from the public, a local man named Isaac Pollard contacted them and said that when he had been passing the premises earlier that day he too had heard the sounds of moaning from within. As he stopped to find out who was making the noise, a man emerged from the building carrying a long slim parcel wrapped in paper. When asked what the noise was, he replied, 'Oh, we just had a bit of bother.' He then returned inside the building only to re-emerge soon after, when he said that 'everything was alright now.' Pollard noticed blood on the man's hands and was able to provide a good description of him, which fitted that of a former employee, John William Ellwood.

Ellwood was a former soldier from Bradford who had been employed at his brother-in-laws dye works as a Clerk. After fourteen years service, he had recently been sacked following a disagreement with his superiors. In the early hours of the following morning Ellwood was arrested in his bed and, the following day, he was placed in an identity parade, where he was recognised by two witnesses. His clothing also had bloodstains on it and, following further investigation, it was found that a man matching Ellwood's description had purchased a poker on the morning of the murder. It was also found that the victim

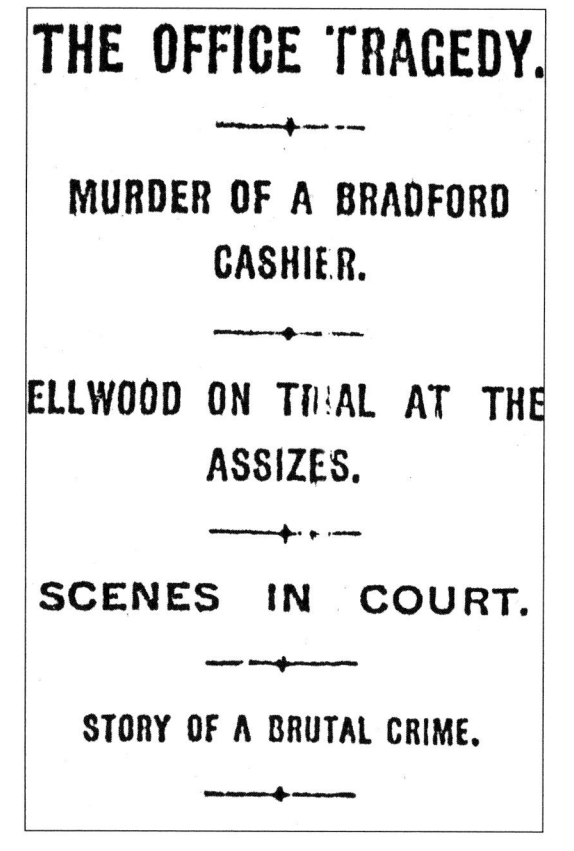

Newspaper account of the Bradford murder. (T.J. Leech Archive)

Hangman Harry Pierrepoint. Ellwood boasted he knew the hangman and would make trouble for him at the execution. (Author's collection)

had given a letter to the office junior to take to Ellwood on the morning of the murder.

At his trial at Leeds Assizes, Ellwood was found guilty of murder and on the 11 November was convicted on strong evidence and sentenced to death by Mr Justice Pickford.

Hangmen Henry and Thomas Pierrepoint, who, like Ellwood, lived in Bradford, were selected to carry out the sentence. Ellwood boasted that he knew Henry and told guards he would give him as much trouble as possible. In the event, the execution was so quick he didn't have time to resist before he was pinioned and led to the scaffold. As he took his place on the drop, Ellwood turned and declared, 'Harry, you're hanging an innocent man.'

35

'AS DEAD AS A MACKEREL'

Thomas Mead, 12 March 1909

On Friday evening, 27 November 1908, 36-year-old Clara Howell and her partner of seven years, 33-year-old labourer Thomas Mead, visited friends before returning to their home at Crook's Yard, Leeds. At a few minutes before midnight, two police officers on duty close to Crook's Yard were alerted to sounds of a disturbance coming from inside one of the houses and hurried to the scene. Seeing it was merely a domestic dispute, they asked the occupants to keep the noise down and left.

An hour later another argument broke out, and there were further disturbances throughout the night. Shortly after daybreak a neighbour saw Thomas Mead leave the house and lock the door behind him. Later that day, Mead called at a neighbour's house and asked him if he could stay the night and while there he confessed that he had killed Clara Howell, telling one of the people at the house that he had left her 'as dead as a mackerel.'

The following morning the body of Clara Howell was discovered; she had been punched and kicked before being battered with a broom handle. A post-mortem found the cause of death as a ruptured intestine.

When Thomas Mead stood before Lord Justice Coleridge in the following February, his defence argued that Mead's mind was so unhinged by drink that he did not know what he was doing, and that he was therefore guilty of manslaughter.

In his summing up, Coleridge said that if the jury were convinced Mead was incapable of forming the intention to kill, they could find a verdict of manslaughter. The jury found him guilty of murder and after conviction his counsel appealed that the trial judge had misdirected the jury on a point about being mad with rage as opposed to insanity, and which they suggested had swayed the jury from returning a verdict of manslaughter. The appeal was dismissed.

36

'FOR THIS PIECE OF PAPER'

John Raper Coulson, 9 August 1910

John Raper Coulson, 4 Springfield Place.
I have murdered my wife and child for this piece of paper having been brought to me at my place of work. She has been nothing but a bitch for some while. This was done on 23th May. You will find me in dam, somewhere about cold dam, Lower Lane.

Note written on the back of summons received by John Coulson, May 1910

At lunchtime on 24 May 1910, following sounds of a fierce quarrel earlier that morning at a house at Dudley Hill, Bradford, neighbours became concerned for the welfare of 29-year-old Jane Ellen Coulson and her 5-year-old son, Thomas. They knew relations between Jane and her 32-year-old husband John had broken down and that on the previous afternoon she had served a summons on him for assault. Coulson worked as a foundry labourer and the summons had been served at his place of work, causing him great embarrassment and anger. Finishing his shift he hurried home and the sound of raised voices quickly followed, which lasted throughout most of the night.

Jane Coulson had spoken briefly to a neighbour at 6 a.m. that morning, and shortly afterwards Coulson left the house. Later that morning, when a neighbour called and received no answer to repeated knocking on her door, and knowing that she had not left the house, the police were called. Receiving no reply to their knocking, officers peered through the windows, and, seeing nothing was amiss, they decided not to force an entry and left.

Leaving his house that morning, Coulson called at a pawnbroker's, where he pledged his wife's wedding ring, and at 11 a.m. he was at work showing workmates the summons he had received on the previous day. On the back Coulson had written the few chilling lines.

That night, in a public house, he showed some friends the same summons. One of them asked what the message on the back meant but Coulson didn't answer. As a result, the friend slipped out of the bar and went to the police. Two officers went back to the house and this time, receiving no answer to their knocking, they forced the door. Inside they found a pitiful sight. The bodies of the Jane and Thomas lay with their throats cut, the mother on the bedroom floor, her son on the adjacent bed. Next to the bodies lay a bloodstained carving knife. Their throats had been cut so savagely that both were almost decapitated. A doctor later put the time of death at around seven that morning. Detectives didn't have to wait long for their suspect. A short time later Coulson returned home, his clothes sodden from a failed attempt to drown himself.

Wife-killer John Raper Coulson. (T.J. Leech Archive)

Tom Pierrepoint carried out his first senior execution at Leeds in 1910. (T.J. Leech Archive)

At his subsequent trial before Lord Chief Justice Coleridge at Leeds on 21 July, Coulson claimed that he had been driven to the attack by his wife's provocation, and offered a plea of manslaughter. Asked to consider their verdict, the jury did not even bother to leave the witness box before announcing they found Coulson guilty of murder.

Coulson's execution marked the debut of a new chief executioner, a role entrusted to fellow Bradfordian Thomas Pierrepoint following the sacking of his brother, Harry, a few weeks before. Harry Pierrepoint's dismissal left the Governor with a problem, as the only other qualified executioners on the list (Ellis and Willis) had been engaged for a job in Newcastle scheduled that same morning. It was a problem he had encountered five years earlier and, as before, he had to call out of retirement William Warbrick of Bolton to act as his assistant.

Coulson was due to hang alongside another man convicted at the same assizes, former soldier Edward Woodcock, who had also cut the throat of the woman he lived with. Woodcock was reprieved on the day before his execution and Coulson went to the gallows alone.

Edward Woodcock hanged himself in his cell three weeks after his sentence had been commuted.

37

ALL OVER A SOVEREIGN

Henry Ison, 29 December 1910

On Saturday afternoon, 23 July 1910, 45-year-old bricklayer's labourer Henry Ison, his common-law wife of the last dozen years, Mary Jenkins, and two of Mary's friends were drinking in the Yorkshire

Hussar Inn, a public house in Leeds. By the early evening, with Ison the worse for drink, they returned to his home at Boynton Street, Quarryhill, where he asked her friends to leave.

A few hours later, Mary was seen running from the house, pursued by Ison. Neighbours saw Ison grab Mary back by her hair, kicking her several times on the legs as he dragged her back inside. The sounds of a quarrel continued for over an hour until they ended in a loud thud.

Later that night, Ison called on Mary's sister. He told her that they had quarrelled and she had better go to the house. When she did, she found Mary lying in a pool of blood, having been battered with a poker. The police soon arrived, having been called by the neighbours, and Ison said it was all over a sovereign. Ison said he had given her the coin, which she told him she had lost. He said he didn't believe her and, deciding to teach her a lesson, he struck her. Mary's injuries were so severe that she died in hospital the following morning.

Ison was tried before Mr Justice Hamilton at Leeds Assizes on 24 November. His defence counsel refuted the confession Ison was alleged to have made and claimed that Mary had died as a result of falling downstairs, pointed out that there were no traces of blood on the poker. They called a doctor, who testified that the injuries were consistent with a fall down a flight of stairs.

The prosecution called another doctor who contradicted this, claiming that the injuries could not have been caused by a fall. The court heard that the couple, although good workers, were both addicted to drink and that Mary often pawned items of his clothes to buy drink, which led to frequent rows. The Crown alleged that the murder was as a result of one of these quarrels. The jury chose to believe the prosecution's version and found Ison guilty of murder, but adding a strong recommendation for mercy. Ison protested his innocence and when asked if he had anything to say before sentence was passed, he said, 'I think it's a very unjust sentence. I am innocent. I am not guilty of murder.'

38

MURDER ON THE FARM

John William Thompson, 27 March 1917

Constitution Farm stood on a remote spot at the top of Constitution Hill, at Molescroft, Beverley, North Yorkshire. The hind and bailiff at the farm was John Henry Tinsdale, who lived there with his wife and four children. Shortly after 1 p.m. on Thursday 15 February 1917, Tinsdale's 13-year-old daughter, Lily, was seen entering the stack yard of the farm, followed a short time later by John Thompson, a 43-year-old shepherd who had worked and lodged at the farm since May of the previous year.

Thompson was conspicuous by his absence that afternoon and when Lily also failed to return to the house at teatime, her parents became worried. John Tinsdale remembered seeing both Thompson and Lily in the stack yard earlier that afternoon and went to look around. His worst fears were soon confirmed when he discovered his daughter's body hidden beneath some straw. Her throat had been cut and her clothing had been disarranged as if the killer had attempted to rape her.

Thompson was arrested when seen wandering the streets of Beverley later that night. His hands and clothing was heavily bloodstained, as were his pipe and a clasp knife. Thompson explained that the blood had been from a sheep he had been tending, but forensic tests found it to be human not sheep blood. A small plug of tobacco had also been found beside the body and a shopkeeper in Molescroft told detectives he had sold an identical piece to Thompson that lunchtime.

TERRIBLE MURDER AT MOLESCROFT.

FATHER'S AWFUL DISCOVERY.

DAUGHTER FOUND DEAD.

HEAD ALMOST SEVERED FROM BODY.

[BY OUR OWN REPORTER]

The annals of crime in Beverley and district contain no darker chapter than the brutal murder in broad daylight on Thursday afternoon of a little girl named Lily Tindale, aged 13½ years, the daughter of a hind named John Henry Tindale, who lives at Constitution Farm, standing on the top of Constitution Hill at Mole-croft, to the north of Beverley. The scene of the crime is a particularly lonely spot, and the farmhouse stands about 200 yards from the roadside. The farm is in the occupation of Mr J. W. Hanson, who resides in Beverley, and the homestead is occupied by his bailiff, Mr John Henry Tindale, father of the victim.

From information received by the police it appears that shortly before four o'clock on aged 43 years, was arrested by Detective Bayley of the Beverley Borough Police Force, who had been requested by the County Constabulary to keep a sharp look out and help them in their quest. The man Thompson, who has been arrested, is single and was employed on the farm. He had lived at the farm-house with Mr and Mrs Tindale for some time, together with three or four other farm hands.

The weapon with which the crime was committed had not up to Thursday night been found. There are a number of drains in the vicinity of the farm, and the police thought that it may have been thrown into one of these.

The man who has been arrested is a native of Bewholme, and had been working in the Beverley

Mr. and Mrs. Tindale and Family.
The deceased girl in this picture is seen as a baby on her mother's knee.

Newscutting describing the Molescroft murder. (T.J. Leech Archive)

SHOCKING TRAGEDY AT A LONELY YORKSHIRE FARM.

Lily Tinsdale's body was discovered covered by straw at the farm. (T.J. Leech Archive)

Tried before Mr Justice McCardie on 9 March at York, Thompson was convicted on overwhelming evidence and after confessing his guilt to the chaplain he was hanged just forty days after committing a brutal and vile murder.

39

JEALOUSY

Robert Gadsby, 18 April 1917

Julia Ann Johnson had been married for twenty-four years when, in 1914, she and her husband separated. Eventually she met and began a relationship with Robert Gadsby, a 65-year-old widower, who worked as a labourer at a dyer's works in Bramley, Leeds. To all who knew them, they appeared to have a loving relationship, although they did not share a home.

Early in 1917, Mrs Johnson's daughter visited her mother, but found the front door locked. As she had expected her to be at home she looked through the window and was horrified to see Gadsby kneeling over the stricken body of her mother, holding a bloodstained knife. She hurried to get help and when the police arrived and broke into the house they apprehended Gadsby and placed him under arrest. Julia Johnson's throat had been cut and she had died from her injuries.

When he stood trial before Mr Justice McCardie at Leeds Assizes on 28 February, Gadsby protested his innocence. He admitted that they had had a terrible row but said that during the struggle the penknife he had in his hands had 'accidentally' cut her throat. When challenged as to why he would be holding a penknife in the first place, he stated that he had been 'cutting some tobacco' moments before the row had started. He said he did not deliberately cut her throat, as he 'loved every hair on her head.'

The prosecution claimed that Gadsby had been consumed by jealousy and had accused Julia of seeing other men. On the morning of the murder he visited her house asking for the return of a ring he had given her some time ago, along with some money he said she owed him. She had denied his accusations of being unfaithful and refused to return the ring, instructing him to remember a promise he had made to her that the ring was a symbol that they would never part. There followed a violent struggle during which he picked up a knife and cut her throat.

After just a short deliberation, the jury found him guilty of wilful murder and he was sentenced to death.

'I am innocent and God is my judge,' Gadsby declared before he was lead from the dock.

40

IN A DRUNKEN RAGE

John William Walsh, 17 December 1918

Ruth Elizabeth Moore had separated from her husband during the early days of the First World War and initially lived alone at her home in the Outwood district of Wakefield. A year later, now aged 37, she began a relationship with John Walsh, a 33-year-old collier who lived across town. The romance soon developed into a full-blown affair and he began to share her home. However, the relationship deteriorated into an unhappy one and the couple took to arguing over the most trivial matter, mainly due to Walsh's intemperate habits.

Despite this, in December 1916, they moved across town to a house on Calder Terrace, with Walsh's brother moving in as a lodger. The change of address did little to stem the quarrelling and following more drunken rows, the lodger packed his bags and moved out.

By the summer of 1918 relations had become so poor that Ruth ordered Walsh out of the house. Walsh packed his bags, but two weeks later, in early July, he returned and, having seemingly made up their differences, was allowed to stay. Within days the arguments started again and Walsh was told to get out.

On Thursday morning, 11 July, Walsh called on the next-door neighbours and asked to speak to the husband. Told he was not home he asked the lady of the house, a Mrs Lockwood, if she had a cigarette, adding, 'I've done it. I have done her in!'

Walsh was advised to give himself up and, finishing his smoke, he headed for the local police station. He told officers that he had entered the house at around 5 a.m. that morning and, finding

The Illustrated Police News *recorded the murder of Ruth Moore. (T.J. Leech Archive)*

Ruth asleep in bed, he had strangled her. 'I can only say that I am guilty and I am willing to swing. It is through sickness. I am upset. That is all I have to say.'

At Walsh's trial in November, his defence counsel suggested that the charge should be one of manslaughter. Medical evidence revealed that the deceased had a history of heart trouble and it had not taken much force or pressure to bring about her death. Walsh had by this time changed his story to say he only grabbed her neck in an attempt to wake her and that she had died accidentally. When this line of defence failed the defence counsel attempted to show he was insane and pointed to the statement made on his arrest, in which he claimed he had carried out the crime while 'sick', suggesting that this sickness was insanity.

The Crown's case was simply that Walsh, in a drunken rage, had killed the woman who had ended their relationship and evicted him from her house. Having been asked to consider the medical evidence and the original confession Walsh had made at the police station, the jury took just a matter of minutes to find him guilty of murder.

'I do not hold out to you any expectation that the sentence would be interfered with by the Crown,' Mr Justice Darling said as he passed sentence, adding that it was as cruel and treacherous a murder as he could recall.

41

AN UNFAITHFUL WIFE

Benjamin Hindle Benson, 7 January 1919

Shortly before the outbreak of the First World War, Charles and Annie Mayne found positions at the home of wealthy Benjamin Hindle Benson at Atkinson Hill, Hunslet. Mayne worked as handyman while his wife took the role of housekeeper. Within a year, 25-year-old Annie and her employer began an affair and when her husband found them in bed together he packed his bags and, after telling Benson he was welcome to her, he walked out.

Annie remained at the house and, although Benson was sixteen years her senior, the couple lived as man and wife for the next year or so until, in 1916, with the fate of the nation in grave danger, Benson, too old for conscription, decided to enlist. After training he was posted to France and with her 'husband' away, Annie took a string of lovers, one of whom was a soldier named Parkin.

She succeeded in keeping her infidelities a secret from Benson until the evening of 26 August 1918, when he arrived home unannounced. Finding the house empty, Benson poured himself a drink and waited for Annie to return. Later that night he heard the key in the door and was horrified to find Annie in the company of Parkin, both the worse for drink. After locking the door she took him by the hand and headed for the bedroom. Benson followed a few minutes later and, pushing open the bedroom door, he found the couple rolling around on his bed.

The young soldier saw the rage in Benson's eyes and fled down the stairs with the older man in hot pursuit. Parkin managed to escape a beating and when Benson returned to the bedroom a heated argument ensued. Two days later Annie received two letters from Parkin. Benson demanded to see them but Annie refused to hand them over. They began another fierce quarrel during which he struck her across the face and threatened to kill her. Wiping the blood from her cheek Annie then mockingly told Benson that she had spent all his money and had no intention of giving up her lover.

Mr Justice Avory sentenced Benjamin Benson to death, the first of four men he sent to the gallows at Leeds. (T.J. Leech Archive)

In a jealous rage, Benson picked up his razor lying next to the kitchen sink and savagely cut her throat. Annie died in hospital shortly afterwards, by which time Benson was already under arrest.

Tried before Mr Justice Avory at Leeds Assizes on Monday 2 December, Benson's defence was one of extreme provocation, but when the background of Benson's affair, which had caused the break-up of the Mayne's marriage, was revealed in court, the prosecution pointed out to the jury the morality of the prisoner.

An appeal was launched following conviction, which debated the same point of extreme provocation. It was quickly rejected with the panel stating that if he was reprieved 'a fortiori' or similar action would have to be taken in the case of any husband who murdered an unfaithful wife.

42

THE DESERTERS

Percy George Barrett & George William Cardwell, 8 January 1919

At 62 years old, widow Rhoda Walker had kept her late husband's silversmith's shop going in her home at Mill Hill Road, Town End, Pontefract. She was a frail woman and being afraid to be alone in the house, she took a lodger, bank clerk Gertrude Lawn. In recent times Mrs Walker had also had a number of staff at the shop but when they were called up to serve in the war, so she continued serving customers alone and tending to repairs in the small workshop on the premises.

At shortly after 2 p.m. on Friday 16 August 1918, Gertrude Lawn left the house to go into Pontefract. When she returned at 4.20 p.m. she found the shop door locked and the front shop window had been disturbed. The adjacent front door was also locked and when she made her way around the back, she found Mrs Walker lying on the kitchen floor.

The old woman had suffered a terrible beating: her clothes were saturated with blood from horrific head wounds. There was a gaping wound in her forehead, a fractured jaw, two black eyes and the fingers on her left hand were broken. Despite the injuries, Mrs Walker was still alive. She was rushed to the local hospital but after drifting in and out of consciousness several times she died in the early hours of Saturday morning.

At the hospital the old woman had given detectives a lead; she muttered several times the phrase, 'Oh, George, don't!' Robbery was clearly the motive; witnesses came forward to say that two men wearing the uniforms of the Army Service Corp (ASC) had been seen loitering outside the shop on the afternoon of the murder. One of the men was sporting six distinctive 'wound stripes', awarded to servicemen injured in battle.

On the following Tuesday the funeral of Mrs Walker took place, and later that day two men were arrested. Investigations by officers in Pontefract had led police to the house of a Mrs Annie Pratt in nearby Ackworth. Annie was the sister of 22-year-old George Walter Cardwell, an army deserter, and further enquires led detectives to London, where Cardwell was arrested along with fellow deserter, 19-year-old Percy George Barrett, as they tried to sell items of jewellery in a public house. The jewellery, some of which was smeared with blood, still bore the price tickets identified as belonging to the murdered woman.

The two deserters stood trial before Mr Justice Avory on 3 December. It lasted less than a day. Both pleaded not guilty, but ignorant of the laws of guilt by association, they condemned themselves by

PONTEFRACT MURDER.

Death Sentence on Two Soldiers.

Judge and His Painful Duty.

At Leeds Assizes, yesterday, before Mr. Justice Avory, George Walter Cardwell (21), of Brighouse, and Percy George Barrett (21), both soldiers, were charged with the murder of Rhoda Walker at Pontefract on Aug. 16. They put in a plea of "not guilty." A further charge of committing robbery with violence was preferred against them, and Barrett pleaded "guilty" to receiving. Mr. Chas. Mellor and Mr. G. F. L. Mortimer prosecuted, and Mr. F. J. O. Codlington and Mr. R. A. Bateman were for the defence.

After a summing up by the Judge lasting an hour and ten minutes, the jury retired at 6.50 p.m. to consider their verdict, the case having lasted since 10.30 a.m. Returning at 6.57 the jury found both prisoners guilty of murder. Asked if they had anything to say why sentence should not be passed, both prisoners protested their innocence. Before passing sentence of death his Lordship said that in a somewhat lengthy experience he had never had a more painful duty to perform than in passing sentence of death on these two youths, but it was a sentence which must inevitably follow upon the crime of which they had been convicted. Each of the prisoners now said he was innocent, but the jury, in his (the Judge's) opinion, had on evidence which left no alternative found that they were both guilty.

News that the two Pontefract murderers had been convicted. (Author's Collection)

each trying to blame the other for the murder. Following his arrest, Barrett had made a statement in which he claimed:

> Cardwell was in the shop when the post woman went in… he hid in the parlour because there was nobody in the shop at the time, and also because he saw the shadow of someone looking through the window… he heard someone coming in through the back way and he made a rush towards the kitchen door, thinking it was a man but it was Mrs Walker. After leaving Ackworth we got a train to Wakefield and arrived at his mother's house about 12 o'clock. He washed his clothes next day which were covered in blood…

Cardwell, a native of Brighouse, gave a different version of events. He said he had been released from Borstal in 1915 after serving a term for stealing from gas meters. He was 17 at the time and in May that year he had joined the colours and gone to France, where he was wounded once and gassed five times. Subsequently passed unfit for service he was transferred to the ASC, but not before he received a recommendation for a DCM and military medal for bravery. He had deserted from his unit because he felt that if he was fit to be in the ASC then he was fit to return to France.

He said that he became friendly with fellow deserter Barrett, and they went to stay with Cardwell's sister at Ackworth and found work at Hemsworth colliery, while they waited to be called-up again. He said that on the day of the murder he had dressed in his uniform and gone to the Pontefract jeweller's to buy a watch key without any intention of committing a crime. Barrett entered the shop and as he waited outside he saw his friend's bloodstained hand reach into the window and snatch some items. Barrett then came out of the shop and said, 'we will have to get away from here. I have killed the old woman.'

This version seemed to be the more likely. A witness had said that they had seen a soldier with wound stripes standing alone outside the shop during the afternoon, but regardless of which version was the truth, as the law stood both were deemed equally as guilty, as, the prosecutor told the court, 'both had been prepared to benefit from a share of the spoils.'

The jury needed just seven minutes before returning a guilty verdict. Awaiting execution, Cardwell penned a last letter to his father stating that he was innocent and had been convicted on a coward's statement.

43

WITH GREAT PROVOCATION?

Lewis Massey, 6 January 1920

In the autumn of 1919, following a short and unhappy marriage, 29-year-old blacksmith Lewis Massey and his wife Margaret, 35, split up. Margaret had lost her first husband during the war and once it was clear that this second marriage was on shaky ground she took out a maintenance order against him on account of his cruelty.

Massey, who also used the name Alfred Hird, was ordered to pay her almost 25s a week, and he at once tried in vain to patch up his broken marriage, making several failed attempts at reconciliation. On Saturday 1 November, he pleaded with Margaret to take him back but as before she refused, and two days later, following threats he had made to her when she failed to take him back, she took out a further summons against him. Still Massey persisted in trying to save his marriage. On Tuesday 4 November he called round and once more pleaded with Margaret to take him back. Again she refused, adding that if he did not leave her alone, she would go back to the police.

The following day, Massey returned to his lodgings in Hunslet Road, Leeds and told fellow lodgers that he had murdered Margaret. He then left his lodgings and went to his sister's, where he was arrested a short time later. Margaret Massey had been battered about the head with a poker and a hatchet; the attack was witnessed by her young daughter, Emily.

Massey told detectives he had gone to see Margaret and found her drinking with her sister. Both women were drunk and began to berate him. They began a quarrel, during which Margaret grabbed a poker from beside the fire and struck him on the head, leaving a large bruise. In a rage he picked up the axe used to chop wood from beside the fire and battered her with it before fleeing as she slumped to the ground.

'Is she dead?' he asked, when officers called at his sister's house. Told she was, he added; 'I am very pleased. I meant to do her in.'

Tried at Leeds Assizes before Lord Chief Justice Coleridge in December, his counsel argued that there was a great deal of provocation and that the victim had wielded the first blow. The prosecution contested the issue of provocation, claiming that there was little if any to justify the savagery of the attack. It was, however, the statement Massey had made following his arrest which painted him as a callous killer who bore no remorse for his actions, and he was condemned after just a short trial.

44

UNDERNEATH THE ARCHES

Miles McHugh, 16 April 1920

Miles McHugh was a 32-year-old man who lived in Chorley, Lancashire with his wife and two children when in January 1918 he separated from his wife and moved to Middlesborough, where he found work as a labourer. Once settled, he continued to send money home to his estranged family while he also formed a relationship with 27-year-old Edith Swainston, who worked as a confectioner's packer.

Edith had recently split with her fiancé but knew nothing of McHugh's wife and family in Lancashire. They began to live together and eventually she found herself pregnant. In March 1919 she gave birth to a child, and although the relationship continued throughout that year, during December she became reacquainted with her former fiancé, a man named Herbert Holman.

When McHugh found out that Edith had been seen talking to Holman he flew into a rage and moved out of their lodgings, despite Edith's plea that there was nothing untoward going on. McHugh regularly visited both Edith and his child at their lodgings, but they were often seen quarrelling.

On Saturday afternoon, 24 January 1920, Edith visited McHugh at his lodgings and both were seen leaving shortly after, at around 5 p.m. Later that same evening, a man spotted what looked like a bundle of discarded clothes under some railway arches near to where he was walking. On closer

Miles McHugh and Edith Swainston. (T.J. Leech Archive)

inspection he saw that it was the body of a young woman, identified as Edith Swainston, her throat having been cut from ear to ear.

Miles McHugh was soon arrested and when questioned he admitted to having been in the archway with Edith where they had been arguing. He said that he had told her of his intentions to return to Lancashire, which she was very unhappy about. He started to walk away when he heard a scream and saw that Edith had tried to kill herself by drawing a knife across her throat several times. McHugh said that he had taken the knife off her and thrown it away and left. He admitted that he had not sought help for his wounded girlfriend.

During the trial at York in March, evidence was given to prove that there was no way that the wound to Edith's neck could have been self inflicted and McHugh was found guilty of murder and sentenced to death by Mr Justice Bailache.

45

PLANS FOR A NEW LIFE

Thomas Hargreaves Wilson, 6 May 1920

Having served his country well during the critical last years of the First World War, forty-five-year-old Thomas Wilson was finally demobbed in the autumn of 1919 and in November he returned to his wife, Annie, and their three daughters, at their home in Kirkstall, Leeds. It was not to be a joyous reunion: the relationship had been under strain for some time due to Wilson's brutal nature, and within weeks they parted. Annie had already accepted that if things didn't work out this time she would take action, and she wasted no time in making matters final by obtaining a separation order and making plans for a new life away from her husband.

On 16 January 1920, Wilson called around to see his estranged wife. Usually when he called around the door was locked and he was unable to gain entry, but today it had been left unlocked and he was able to let himself inside. From the moment he arrived it was clear he was spoiling for an argument. He asked for a receipt for the maintenance money he had paid her and began to accuse her of seeing another man. When she refused to deny the accusation he picked up a knife from the kitchen table and waved it around threateningly. His eldest daughter tried to pacify him, but it served to cause him to channel his anger against her. As he turned on his daughters they fled upstairs, locking themselves into a bedroom. As Wilson hammered on the door, the girls escaped through the bedroom window and rushed off to find a policeman.

When police officers arrived at the house, they found all the doors and windows locked. When no one answered the door, one of the officers smashed a window and entered the house, where a wild-eyed Wilson brandishing a knife confronted him. Drawing his truncheon, the officer lashed out, knocking the man to the ground. A search of the house uncovered the body of Annie Wilson lying beneath a bed; with horrific head injuries and her throat cut. Medical assistance was summoned but she died before help arrived.

At Leeds Assizes before Mr Justice Roche on 18 March, it was found that Wilson had used an axe on his victim before cutting her throat with a razor, allegedly because she had taken out a separation order against him. He offered a plea of insanity but it failed when officers at Leeds, who had observed Wilson on remand, testified there was no sign of any insanity.

46

MURDER ON THE DANCEFLOOR

Edwin Sowerby, 30 December 1920

'Me and Janie gone for ever – E. Sowerby. Love to all.'

Note written by Edwin Sowerby, 26 October 1920

Although they had parted almost six months earlier, 28-year-old miner Edwin Sowerby could not get over his break-up with 19-year-old Jane Darwell. Sowerby had been courting Jane, a domestic servant who lived with her parents on the same street as Sowerby at Crofton, a small mining village on the outskirts of Wakefield, since the turn of the year, but by the summer she had tired of the romance.

Sowerby took the news badly and began to pester her, even asking her father, who worked alongside him at Walton Pit, to interfere, but he told Sowerby he was unwilling or unable to get involved. On Saturday 23 October 1920, Sowerby bumped into Jane's father and again asked if he would 'talk to Janie.' Again her father refused to intervene.

The Illustrated Police News *sketch of the murder of Jane Darwell. (T.J. Leech Archive)*

MURDER ON THE DANCEFLOOR

On the following Monday, Crofton Cricket Club was holding a 'whist drive and dance' at the local village hall, a few yards from Sowerby and Janie's homes. Knowing that Jane would be there, Sowerby bought a programme and was in the hall when the drive ended and the dance began. The first dance was a set of Lancers, one needing a dance partner, and when Jane's friend opted to sit out of the dance, Sowerby spied his chance and approached. The bell announcing the start of the dance rang, but instead of accepting his request, she whispered something to him, at which Sowerby pulled out a razor and slashed her across the throat, spraying blood across a number of people sat beside the dancefloor. As Jane slumped to the floor he pulled the razor across his own throat, but succeeded in only causing superficial injuries.

Police were soon at the scene and as Sowerby was led away he handed his programme to a friend and showed him the note he had scribbled in pencil at the bottom. 'Read it aloud for all to hear,' he shouted to his friend as he was escorted out of the hall and into an ambulance.

Jane had died almost immediately. Her mother, sitting at home by the fire, heard the screams as the fatal act was played out; unaware her daughter was involved. Sowerby was taken to Clayton Hospital, where his wounds were patched up sufficiently for him to stand trial before Mr Justice Slater at Leeds Assizes just five weeks later. The defence was based around the sanity of the prisoner, who had been visited by a doctor several times in the weeks prior to the murder after Sowerby had been complaining of headaches and lack of sleep. Sowerby's mother told the court that her son had been suffering from pains in his head following his discharge from the army in 1918.

Shortly before the murder, Sowerby told a number of his friends that he intended doing away with himself, telling one that he intended putting his head on a railway line if he failed to get Jane back.

The trial lasted less than a day and after a deliberation of twenty minutes, the jury, believing the prosecution's version of events, that Sowerby, a lover spurned had committed murder through jealousy and had then tried to end his own life. They dismissed the claims of insanity, stating that the prisoner had been fully aware of his actions while committing the crime.

Sowerby neglected to appeal and three weeks later he walked bravely to the scaffold, carrying a photograph of his former sweetheart in his pocket.

Official notification of the execution of Edwin Sowerby. (T.J. Leech Archive)

47

MURDER AT THE CHINESE LAUNDRY

Lee Doon, 5 January 1923

Sing Lee was a successful businessman who, since he had arrived in England at the age of 25, had built up a lucrative laundry business, owning several properties in Liverpool and a laundry on Crookes Road, Sheffield. He was a well-respected member of the Chinese community and was frequently sought out for his advice. The laundry in Sheffield was where he chose to base himself and he lived above the shop, along with one of his employees, 27-year-old Lee Doon. Another employee, Lily Siddall, managed the accounts and paperwork and had worked for Lee for a number of years.

On 9 September 1922, Lee asked Lily if she could do some extra hours the following day, a Sunday, to help clear a backlog of work. She was happy to do this and arranged to come around the following morning.

When she arrived the next day she was greeted by Lee Doon, who said that Sing Lee had returned to China, leaving instruction that Doon was now in charge. Mrs Siddall found this difficult to believe, as Lee had not mentioned a planned visit to China. She kept her doubts to herself though and carried on with her work, but on the following day, Lily's suspicions were heightened when Doon engaged workmen to dig a hole in the cellar floor. When she challenged Doon about why they were digging a large hole, he said that it was none of her business.

Lily's uncertainties grew when a lady friend of Lee's came to the shop asking after him. She said that they had made arrangements to meet the previous evening but he had failed to turn up, which was totally out of character. Deciding that she needed to get to the bottom of the mystery, Lily started asking around among Lee's friends and acquaintances to see if anyone knew of his whereabouts or indeed of his intentions to travel to China. She even sent a telegram to the laundry in Liverpool asking if Lee was there, only to receive a reply that he wasn't.

Deciding to take matters into her own hands she travelled to Liverpool, where she met with Lee's cousin, Sun Kwong Lee, with whom she shared her worries. He immediately agreed to accompany her back to Sheffield where they went straight to the police to report Sing Lee missing.

When police went to the laundry on Crookes Road, initially they could get no answer, but after much hammering on the door, it was eventually answered by Lee Doon. Asked where his boss was, he said he'd gone away. Police searched the building and in the cellar they found a large pile of coal in the middle of the floor over the recently dug hole. Taking up spades, they moved the coal and discovered what appeared to be a freshly dug grave covered in earth. Digging further, they came across a metal trunk and inside were the battered remains of Sing Lee.

At his trial before Mr Justice Greer in December, Doon said that he had accidentally murdered Lee during a violent quarrel. He had discovered Lee taking drugs and had tried to stop him, and in the resulting scuffle he hit Lee in self-defence. To his horror he found that he had killed him and had decided the only way out was to tell friends and acquaintances that Lee had gone away whilst secreting the body in the cellar. A post-mortem, however, revealed a very different version of events. Lee had been strangled and bludgeoned many times.

In the face of overwhelming evidence, Doon was found guilty and sentenced to death.

The laundry at Crookes, Sheffield, where Sing Lee was murdered. (T.J. Leech Archive)

48

'I BELIEVE IT IS MURDER'

John William Eastwood, 28 December 1923

John Clarke was a 48-year-old pot man and bartender working at the Bay Horse Inn on Daniel Street, Sheffield. The landlord and landlady were 39-year-old John Eastwood and his wife, Ethel, and for some time Eastwood had become suspicious about his wife's relationship with Clarke, whom he felt was becoming far too familiar and over-friendly with her.

Matters came to a head in June 1923 when Eastwood left his wife and went to Blackpool with a married lady friend, Mildred Parramore, staying for nearly two weeks before returning to Sheffield, where he took lodgings. When he returned to Sheffield he had tried to rebuild his relationship with his wife but she would not take him back. After he had left her, Mrs Eastwood took over as sole landlady at the Bay Horse.

Early on the morning of 29 July, Eastwood stumbled into the bedroom of his landlord, carrying an axe and declaring that he was going to find Clarke and 'knock him up'. He then threw his door key down, stating that he wouldn't need it any more, and left the lodgings.

Shortly after, Eastwood arrived at Clarke's lodgings, where he awoke Clarke from his sleep by throwing pebbles at his window. When Clarke saw who was making the noise, he went downstairs and let Eastwood in; unaware that he was in any danger. When Mrs Clarke, who was still upstairs in bed, heard the sounds of a struggle, she rushed downstairs to find Eastwood leaving and her husband lying on the floor with terrible head wounds. Clarke was rushed to the hospital, but died the following day.

John Eastwood gave himself up immediately after committing the crime to a policeman, to whom he admitted, 'I believe it is murder, in fact, I'm sure it is.'

He stood trial at the West Yorkshire Assizes in early December 1923, before Mr Justice Talbot. Eastwood's defence claimed that his mind was unbalanced at the time of the attack and that there was a history of mental illness in his family. Both his father and uncle had died in an asylum. The prosecution, however, presented medical evidence to show that Eastwood was not insane, and the jury found him guilty of murder and he was sentenced to death.

49

THE GIGOLO

William Horsley Wardell, 18 June 1924

'Gentleman, private income £1000, desires correspondence, lady, means, private, genuine.'

William Wardell saw himself as something of a gigolo, able to use his undoubted charm on the more affluent women in his hometown of Bradford. Placing the above notice in newspapers, he flitted from one wealthy conquest to the next, but always returned to his fiancée of thirteen years, Ellen Westcott, who ran a Bradford boarding house.

It was under the name of George Goodson that 47-year-old Wardell had wooed Elizabeth Reaney, a widow with wealth and property. After a short but intensive courtship, by the end of 1923 she had agreed to sell her house on Sunderland Road and move with him to a new home in Derbyshire. She had agreed with the vendors to give vacant possession on 23 February 1924. Wardell soon informed his bride-to-be that he had found their ideal home, a cottage in Buxton, and they speeded up the sale of her house.

Neighbours saw Elizabeth at around 10 p.m. on the Friday night, 22 February, standing on her doorstep and peering up and down the street as if waiting for someone. The following morning, removal men called at the house expecting to collect furniture for transportation to Buxton. They were surprised to find a note pinned to the door stating, 'had to go to Buxton' and advising them to return on the Monday. Just as they were leaving, the new owners arrived and, worried by the change of plans, decided to force the door. To their horror they discovered the body of Elizabeth Reaney in the cellar: she had been battered to death with a coal hammer.

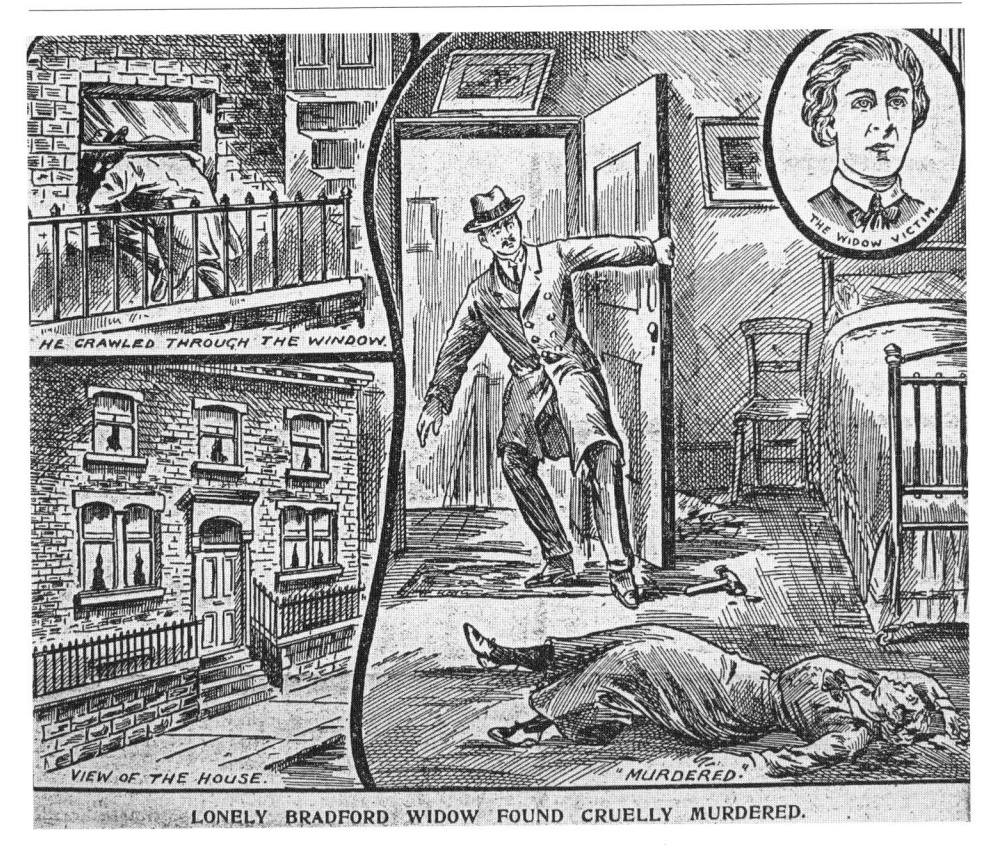

How the Illustrated Police News *recorded the murder of Mrs Reaney. (T.J. Leech Archive)*

William Wardell. (T.J. Leech Archive)

A search of the house revealed a quantity of money, but more telling were four letters, signed by a Mr Goodson at an address in Leeds. Both the name and address were false, but a description of a man led the police to the name of William Wardell.

Wardell was a regular in Peel Inn, Bradford, where he was known as 'Collar Tom' on account of the high shirt collars he sported, and he had been drinking there on the Friday night, leaving at around 10.15 p.m. On the following Wednesday evening, Wardell again visited the Peel Inn, where he was told by the landlord and his friend that the police had been in looking for him. Reluctantly, Wardell agreed to go to the police station to clear his name.

Already known to police as a man of bad character, when interviewed at length and searched, detectives found thirteen treasury notes from the same batch as those found at the murder scene, and Wardell's handwriting matched that on the four letters found at Sunderland Road. The most damning piece of evidence was a notebook found in Wardell's pocket. On one page was the name Elizabeth Reaney, which had the Sunderland Road address, and next to it he had written 'Goodson… Leeds'.

Elizabeth Reaney, conned and murdered by William Wardell. (T.J. Leech Archive)

Tried at West Riding Assizes, Leeds, before Mr Justice Avory in May, the evidence against Wardell was largely circumstantial. There were no bloodstains on any of his clothes, and his explanation as to how he had come about the money found in his possession could not be supported. The jury, however, believed the prosecution had built up a strong case against him and found Wardell guilty as charged.

50

'A LOT OF BOTHER WITH A WOMAN'

Alfred Davis Bostock, 3 September 1925

Elizabeth Maud Sherratt believed her lover when he told her that his marriage was all but over and that he was just waiting for the right moment to seek a divorce. The attractive 24-year-old, who had also used the surname Burton, had met her boyfriend, 25-year-old Alfred Bostock, early in 1925, when she found employment as a secretary at the Parkgate Iron Works at Rawmarsh, Rotherham, where Bostock worked as a crane driver.

They soon became clandestine lovers, meeting in secret several times a week. So eager was Bostock to keep the affair a secret that following a comment by a workmate about Bostock and the pretty secretary, that he persuaded her to find another job away from the gossiping tongues of work colleagues.

She agreed and took a job as an usherette at the Parkgate Electra Picture Palace and they continued their relationship into the spring, when she revealed to Bostock she was expecting his child. If she expected this would be the spur for him to end his marriage and set up a home with her and their child, she was cruelly and sadly mistaken.

On Sunday morning, 3 May, the body of Elizabeth Sherratt was discovered floating in the River Don at Rawmarsh. From bloodstains on the footpath it appeared there had been a struggle, which had ended with the killer fracturing her skull with a blunt instrument, before throwing her lifeless body into the murky waters.

Once her identity had been revealed, officers searched her lodgings and discovered many intimate love letters from Bostock. He initially denied knowing the dead woman but later admitted they had been lovers and that he had met up with her briefly on the night before her death. Bostock claimed they had met up early on the Saturday night and after they had parted he spent the evening in several local pubs. Nobody could vouch for his alibi and one workmate told police Bostock had confided in him that he was having 'a lot of bother with a woman', and that 'if I don't do her in this weekend my name isn't Bostock!'

Tried before Mr Justice Finlay on Friday 24 July, and faced with a strong case by the prosecution, the jury needed just fifteen minutes to find Bostock guilty. Asked if he had anything to say before sentence was passed, he replied, 'I am innocent my Lord, and if the dead girl's lips could only speak, they would tell you the same.'

Rotherham killer Alfred Bostock. (T.J. Leech Archive)

51

THE SHEFFIELD HOOLIGANS

Wilfred Fowler, 3 September 1925, & Lawrence Fowler, 4 September 1925

The Fowler Gang, a group of a dozen of so young 'hooligans', had a fearsome reputation throughout Sheffield and in particular in the Attercliffe area of the city. To most citizens they were to be avoided if at all possible, but to one or two men their threats and intimidation held no fear. William Francis

Wilfred Fowler. (T.J. Leech Archive)

Lawrence Fowler. (T.J. Leech Archive)

'Jock' Plommer, murdered by the Fowler Gang. (T.J. Leech Archive)

'Jock' Plommer, a 40-year-old ex-boxer, was one such man and he had already had a number of run-ins with the gang, led by 25-year-old Lawrence Fowler and his 23-year-old brother, Wilfred.

Plommer had already come to blows with one of the Fowler Gang when he had intervened during a brawl in a public house, and given the young thug a beating. On Sunday 26 April 1925, Plommer and another ex-boxer ran into Wilfred Fowler and two more of his gang in another public house and again a fight broke out, and as before it was the hooligans who came off worse. The fight was short and savage and ended with Wilfred being carried out unconscious and with his friends threatening revenge.

Reprisals took place the following day. Plommer was sitting in the front room of his home when his 10-year-old son rushed in and said that there was a gang outside looking for him. Plommer put down his newspaper and went to confront them. As he walked outside he came face to face with nine members of the gang, including both Fowler brothers, with Wilfred sporting a bandage around his head as a result of the beating on the previous evening.

In an instant they set upon Plommer. Lawrence was the first to make a move, lashing out at the older man with a heavy poker and sending him crashing to the ground. The others closed in, attacking the stricken man with chains, knives and clubs, and kicking him with heavy boots as he rolled around the ground defenceless. With their anger sated the gang stepped back, allowing Plommer to stagger home. Rushed to hospital, it was found he had been stabbed in the abdomen and he died in hospital later that day.

Although there had been many witnesses to the attack and detectives knew who the killers were, they faced a problem getting people to make statements for fear of intimidation and reprisals. Eventually, police managed to get people to talk and a total of eleven arrests were made.

With the gang behind bars, their reign of terror quickly crumbled. The dead man's funeral procession was watched by thousands of locals who lined the streets from his home to the local church, and the feeling locally was that his brave stance in facing up to the Fowlers should not be in vain. Soon the police had many statements helping them build up a strong case against the gang.

At the trial before Mr Justice Finlay at the end of July, the brothers remained defiant; believing their rule of fear would prevent witnesses speaking against them. They could only watch from the dock as witness after witness stepped into the dock, one of whom told the court that moments before Plommer was attacked he heard Lawrence say to the boxer, 'You've done our kid and now we'll do for you!'

Counsel for the defence tried in vain to suggest that the gang had merely attacked in self-defence after Plommer had made to assault them, but it was a forlorn hope. Their trial lasted four days, during which time four of the accused were discharged. Of the remaining seven, two were

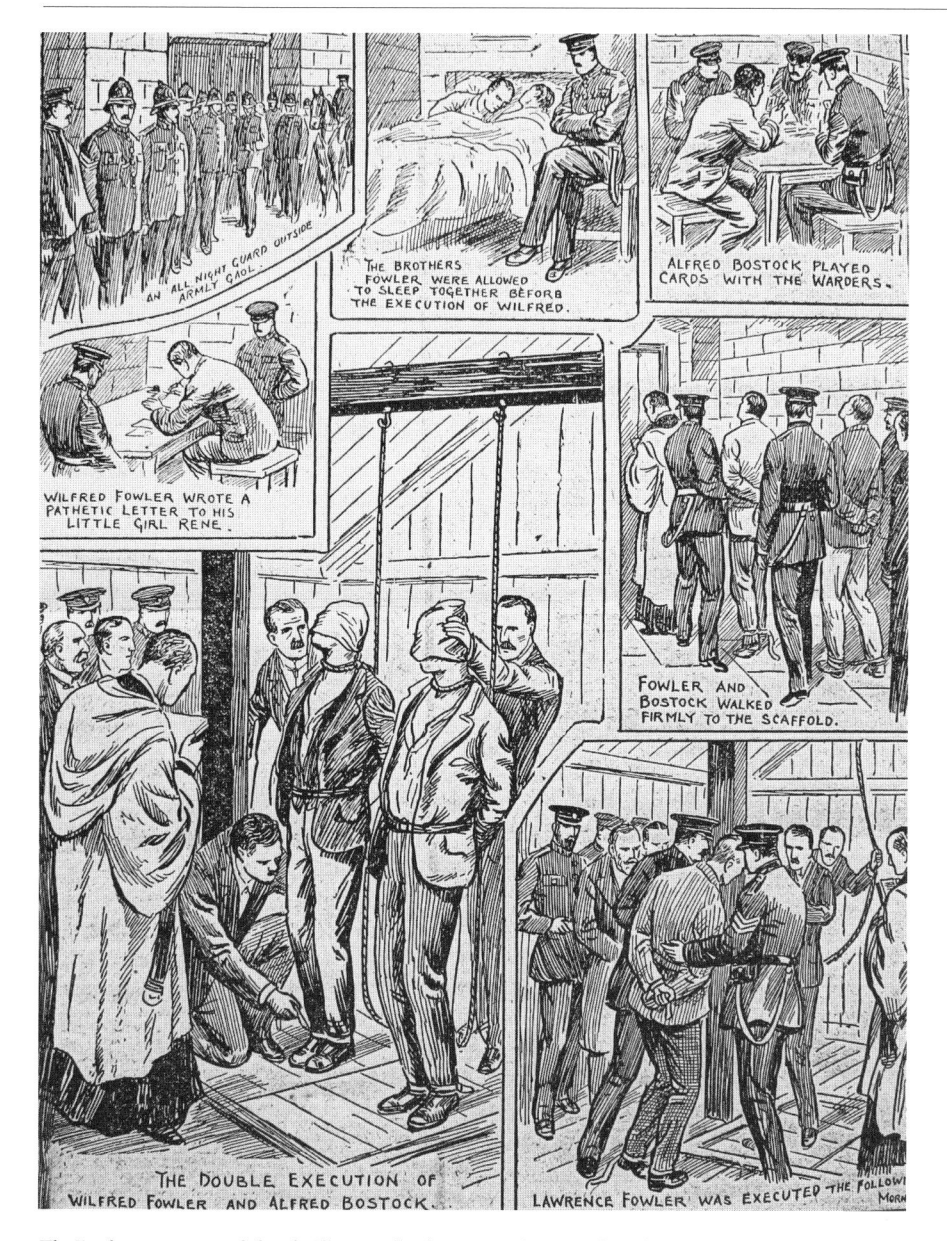

The Fowler case, as recorded in the Illustrated Police News. *(T.J. Leech Archive)*

found not guilty; three were found guilty of manslaughter and received sentences ranging between seven and ten years, while the Fowler brothers were both found guilty of murder and sentenced to death.

It was not clear which of the brothers had caused the fatal knife wound and neither made any confession while awaiting execution. It was decided that they would not be hanged together, instead Wilfred would hang alongside Rotherham killer Alfred Bostock (*see* Chapter 50), with his brother following them to the gallows the next day.

In a rare moment of compassion, Lawrence was allowed to sleep alongside his brother on the night before the execution, being removed to his own cell a few hours before the hangman called.

52

YET ANOTHER DISAGREEMENT

Lorraine Lax, 7 January 1926

Lorraine Lax, a 38-year-old miner, and his wife Elizabeth, known as Lizzie, had been married for over five years and had three children. Their marriage, however, was volatile and unhappy and they frequently argued and separated, largely due to Lax's love of gambling and drink and the resultant concerns about money.

In March 1923, Mrs Lax left her husband following yet another disagreement and moved into new lodgings on Ripon Street, Sheffield, close to where her sister Alice and brother-in-law Henry Antcliffe lived. By the end of the 1924 though, Lizzie and her husband had patched up their differences and he moved back in with his wife and family at Ripon Street.

During August the following year the relationship had once more deteriorated and on 31 August 1925 the situation reached a terrible climax. At 6.45 a.m. there was an urgent knocking at Alice's door. The Lax's landlady wanted Alice and her husband to 'attend' to Lizzie, who was in a bad way in her lodgings. As Henry Antcliffe rushed to Lax's lodgings he spotted Lorraine Lax nearby, who shouted, 'it's no use, she's dead. I'm going to give myself up'. When Antcliffe reached the house he found Lizzie Lax dead, having had her throat cut.

At his trial before Mr Justice Fraser, Lax stated that he had not intended to kill Lizzie and pleaded self-defence. He said that when he got up from his bed that morning, he had accidentally disturbed the sleeping Lizzie, who grew very angry at being woken. There followed a scuffle during which, he claimed, Lizzie drew a knife on him. He said that she cut him with the knife and he did have superficial wounds to his neck. Lax said he then managed to wrestle the knife from her and cut her throat with it 'in the heat of the moment'.

The prosecution produced evidence that the injuries to his neck could have been self-inflicted. In a last desperate attempt to escape the gallows, Lax's defence pleaded insanity, claiming that the prisoner's nerves had been shattered when he had been wounded during the war.

Loraine and Elizabeth Lax. (T.J. Leech Archive)

> **LAX EXECUTED.**
>
> **His Last Letter to His Mother.**
>
> **REQUEST FOR "A PRAYER."**
>
> Lorraine Lax was executed at Armley Gaol, Leeds, yesterday morning, for the murder of his wife, Elizabeth Lax, on August 31st last, at lodgings in Ripon Street, Attercliffe, Sheffield.

Lax's execution made the headlines of the local papers. (T.J. Leech Archive)

The jury were unconvinced and found him guilty of murder. Asked if he had anything to say before sentence was passed on him, Lax said simply, 'No, only I'm extremely sorry.'

53

A FATAL BULLET

William Cornelius Jones, 5 January 1927

After less than six months of marriage, 18-year-old Winifred Jones packed her bags and went back to her mother's. Twenty-one-year-old William Jones, a bricklayer's labourer, and Winifred had married on 31 October 1925 but their short married life was not a happy one. After first living in a caravan they took possession of a house on Crib Lane, Halifax in February of the following year.

In the spring of 1926 Winifred tired of her husband's cruelty and ill treatment and, after returning to her mother's, she contacted a solicitor who wrote to Jones warning that he faced legal proceedings unless he altered his ways. The letter seemed to work, Jones apologised to his wife, she accepted and moved back to Crib Lane, where, within a few weeks, she announced she was pregnant.

The reconciliation was short-lived however, and on 7 July she again packed her bags and went to see a solicitor, who drafted another letter to Jones. This time he told Jones that as his wife was due to give birth, he must keep away until after her confinement, at which time maintenance payments would be discussed. The letter arrived on 10 July and Jones, together with his mother, stormed into the solicitor's office and claimed that his wife was lying about his treatment of her and he was refusing to discuss any thoughts of maintenance payments.

Jones said he intended to initiate proceedings again for spreading falsehoods and leaving the office he returned home to change into his Territorial Army uniform as his unit were due to attend a session on a local rifle range. Once changed, he called at the local drill hall where the quartermaster issued rifles, and then in the company of his colleagues he made his way to the range. En-route Jones spied his wife talking to a friend and although they saw him they did not speak, and despite heading in the

William Jones murdered his wife Winifred at Halifax. (Author's collection)

same direction they stayed on opposite sides of the road. Jones then told his friends he would catch them up and skirted down a side street, only to appear at the far end, and as Winifred approached he dropped down on one knee, took aim and fired. A single shot rang out and Winifred Jones fell to the ground, dying from her injuries before help could arrive.

Taken into custody Jones claimed that the shooting was an accident, and he maintained this when he stood trial before Mr Justice McCardie at Leeds Assizes in December. The prosecution refuted any thoughts of an accident and claimed that he had told colleagues in the Territorial Army that he was angry at the solicitor's letter he had received, and that he intended to shoot his wife. They called witnesses who had seen Jones squat down and aim his rifle as his wife approached, and from the quartermaster who said that the guns had been checked before issue and all had been empty of ammunition.

His defence maintained that it was an accident and that Jones had dropped his rifle, which had gone off accidentally, striking his wife. Refuting this, counsel for the Crown asked the jury to believe that an empty rifle had accidentally fallen from the prisoners hand and discharged a fatal bullet, that had flown across the street and quite by chance struck, among all the people passing down the street, the one person Jones was angry with. The jury agreed and took just a matter of minutes to declare that Jones had wilfully murdered his wife.

54

THE END OF AN AFFAIR

Arthur Harnett, 2 September 1927

Late on the night of 3 May 1927, 27-year-old miner and semi-pro footballer Arthur Harnett left the house of Robert and Isabella Moore at Hemsworth, Yorkshire. He then called into the Blue Bell Hotel, where he shared a drink with an old friend. Harnett tried to sell him a watch, and as he showed it, his friend noticed blood on his hands.

Asked where the blood had come from, Harnett said that he had been involved in a fight earlier that evening, and when his friend chose not to buy the watch, Harnett then said he could have it for

Arthur Harnett's appeal was unsuccessful. (T.J. Leech Archive)

nothing. Harnett then took out some medals from his pocket and passed them to his friend, asking him to keep them safe, adding that he wouldn't need them anymore. He then lowered his eyes and, speaking quietly, confessed that he had killed a woman and was going to the police.

Later that night, he entered a local police station and confessed that he had committed murder. Harnett told officers that he was a frequent caller at the house when 34-year-old Isabella Moore's husband was at work. Although her husband knew of these visits, Harnett had previously reassured him that they were old friends and not having an affair. Suspecting that they were, Moore had told Harnett to stay away, and that night Harnett had gone round to try to get Isabella to leave her husband and run away with him. He had failed in his request, and in a rage he had cut her throat with a razor he had taken to the house.

Harnett pleaded insanity at his trial before Mr Justice MacKinnon at Leeds Assizes in July. The prosecution refuted any claims of insanity by referring to the confession Harnett had made when he surrendered to the police following the murder. Approaching the station he had come upon PC Sagar, a man he knew quite well.

'Take me inside Sagar. I have done something serious,' he said, approaching the officer, and once inside he confessed that he had cut a woman's throat in Westgate. Although he gave no motive for what he had done, and this was used by the defence to support their claims that he was insane, the judge advised the jury that a motive is not necessary for a verdict of murder and despite his plea of insanity, Arthur Harnett was found guilty as charged.

55

A FRIEND OF THE FAMILY

Samuel Case, 7 January 1928

The police investigation into the murder of 24-year-old Mary Alice Mottram lasted less than twenty-four hours. Late on the night of Thursday 20 October 1927, George Mottram finished his shift at Tinsley Park Colliery and returned to his home on Ravencarr Road, Sheffield. Arriving home he

INTAKE MURDERER EXECUTED.

SAMUEL CASE PAYS THE PENALTY.

The Sheffield murderer, Samuel Case, was hanged at 9 o'clock this morning in Armley Gaol, Leeds, for the murder of Alice Mary Mottram, on the Manor Estate, Sheffield, on 20 October.

ONE or two people assembled outside the gaol as early as 7.30, an hour and a half before the execution was timed to take place, and just before nine o'clock there would be about 50 people in two groups assembled in Gloucester terrace, which leads to the gaol.

At nine o'clock the men bared their heads and the group stood in silence

Samuel Case.

Samuel Case was hanged for the murder of his wife's best friend. (T.J. Leech Archive)

found the house unusually quiet and, entering the kitchen, he noticed a half-eaten meal on the table, next to the book his wife had been reading. When he stepped inside the room he recoiled in horror at the sight of his wife, Mary, lying on the kitchen floor, a piece of clothesline knotted tightly around her neck.

Police enquiries soon pointed to 24-year-old miner and family friend Samuel Case. The Case and Mottram families had been close friends since childhood, and Mary Mottram had even been a bridesmaid at Case's wedding. Case said that he and Mary had been having an affair and on the night she died she had told him that she was pregnant by him. He said that Mary was so upset with the situation she found herself in that she asked him to help her kill herself. Case said he had then picked up a tea towel, strangled her with it, and then knotted a clothesline around her neck before fleeing.

On 17 November, days before Case stood trial at Leeds Assizes, there was a sensational development when a prisoner on remand in Manchester confessed to the crime. Liverpudlian William Hartle, an inmate at Strangeways Gaol, claimed that he had murdered Mary Mottram. Interviewed by detectives in Sheffield, Hartle said that he and Case had walked from Liverpool to Sheffield, where they had entered the house, and as Case spoke to the woman Hartle had strangled her.

The confession, though matching many of the known facts, was full of holes. Much of it did not match the evidence gathered at the scene, his knowledge of the layout of the room was inconsistent and, crucially, Hartle's description of Case did not suggest he knew the suspected killer.

In light of this now seemingly false confession, the trial went ahead, and on 29 November 1927 Case appeared before Mr Justice Roche. The prosecution disputed Case's story that he was having an affair with the murdered woman, instead they suggested that on the night of the murder Case had gone to the house and had made some remark or indecent proposal which Mary had rebuked, and when she threatened to tell her husband he had killed her.

56

ABSENT WITHOUT LEAVE

Arthur Leslie Raveney, 14 August 1929

Tuesday 14 May 1929 broke as a warm sunny morning as an armed military escort made its way back to Catterick Army Camp. Up front in the Crossley Military Tender were Sergeants Brett and Prangnell, of the 4th Battalion Tank Corp, while in the back sat the prisoner, 24-year-old Private Arthur Leslie Raveney, picked up for being absent without leave, and his guard Private Leslie White.

As the tender passed through the picturesque village of Constable Burton, Leyburn, Sergeant Prangnell heard a sound that he took to be a blown tyre and told the driver to slow down. At that moment Sergeant Brett looked through his rear window and saw the prisoner running down the road in the direction they had just travelled, while in the back of the tender Private White lay seriously wounded.

'He has shot me,' White whispered, before lapsing into unconsciousness. Prangnell drove the cab back to Leyburn, where a local doctor assessed the wounded man. Seeing he had a severe abdomen wound, the doctor suggested they would be better returning to the Catterick Camp Hospital, where Private White died shortly after arrival.

Police officers from as far away as York were despatched to the area in case Raveney had gone to ground close by. The hunt for the killer lasted seven hours, during which time Raveney discarded his tunic and cap and was seen by witnesses vaulting fences with the skill of 'an Olympic hurdler'. Eventually, Raveney succumbed to exhaustion and as darkness prevailed a posse of over thirty armed officers and civilians cornered the fugitive at Rockwith Quarry, near Newton-le-Willows. He was taken to Leyburn police station and charged with murder.

An inquest found that White had died from gunshot wounds that had punctured both the liver and kidney. 'I am of the opinion that the cause of death was haemorrhage following loss of blood due to a bullet wound,' concluded the pathologist at the inquest.

Raveney's trial at York Assizes before Mr Justice MacKinnon, on Monday 9 July 1929, was little more than a formality. The court heard that there had been bad feeling between the prisoner and the victim which seemed to have stemmed from an incident earlier that year when Raveney, acting as an officer's servant, had been transferred back to ordinary duties after a 'trifling offence' and this had resulted in the prisoner cold-bloodedly shooting his guard while attempting to escape.

Describing events on the day of the shooting, the prosecuting counsel said that Raveney was being transferred back to camp having been picked up as an absentee from his unit by police in Bedale. He had been searched by

Private Arthur Raveney. (Author's collection)

How the Illustrated Police News *covered the murder of Private White. (T.J. Leech Archive)*

police officers at Bedale but no weapon was found on him, although the officer who had conducted the search was forced to admit in court that he had made only a frisk of his pockets, and if the weapon had been concealed under his armpit, as had been suggested, then it would have gone undetected.

In his defence, Raveney claimed that they had travelled some distance in the rear of the lorry when he became cramped and tried to change position. White made some remark about trying to escape, to which the prisoner replied that if had wanted to escape he could have done so by now.

'I was putting my hand in my overcoat pocket to get a cigarette when I looked around at White and saw that he drawn his revolver and that it was loaded,' Raveney claimed. White was alleged to have snarled, 'If you try that you will have some of this coming,' indicating his revolver.

'I was astonished and realised that I was in a dangerous position,' Raveney continued. 'White's hand was shaking so much and with the least pressure, with the gun cocked, I felt it would go off. With my left hand I brushed the revolver lightly aside and grabbed White's right hand. At the same moment I grabbed the barrel and turned it away, but at that moment the van went around a corner and we swayed together. It was here that the gun went off.' Retiring to consider their verdict, the jury believed the prosecution's version of events that Raveney had shot White with the gun he had concealed upon him, rather than the guard's own gun.

57

THE MONEYLENDER

Frederick Gill, 4 February 1931

Frederick Gill was a 26-year-old trolley-bus driver from Keighley who loved to spend money but was very bad at saving it. He regularly borrowed money against forthcoming wages from a local moneylender named Oliver Preston. Gill had a fiancée who had become accustomed to him spending lots of money on her and increasingly he found it difficult to pay his debts. He was in arrears with his rent payments as well as being behind in his debt repayments to Oliver Preston, who had issued a summons against him for unpaid debts.

A barber rented rooms in the same building as Preston's moneylending offices on Station Parade, Keighley and frequently went into the offices in order to read the gas meter, which the two businesses shared. On 25 July 1930, he entered the premises and discovered Preston lying stricken on a couch covered in blood. His desk had been ransacked and his trouser pockets had been turned out. A bloodstained iron bar was also found. Although badly injured and unconscious, he was still alive, and was rushed to hospital. He never recovered from his injuries and died four days later.

The police set out to find the murderer and several witnesses came forward to say that they had seen a man they recognised as Fred Gill leaving Preston's office on the night of the 25 July, at around 6.15 p.m. Preston was known to be in possession of a large amount of money, which was now missing.

Gill was tracked down to Whitehaven, where he had very recently taken his fiancée for a holiday. It was established that Gill had been

Fred Gill.
(T.J. Leech Archive)

Murderer Fights

EXECUTION DELAYED FOR 15 MINUTES.

GRIM SCENE.

Man Who Killed Aged Moneylender.

Fred Gill, the 26-year-old murderer of a Keighley moneylender, put up a fight for life on the way to the scaffold at Armley Prison, Leeds, this morning, and his execution was delayed for some time.

After being taken from the condemned cell, Gill is said to have put up some resistance, and it was not until a quarter-of-an-hour after the usual time that the formal notice of his execution was posted outside the prison.

The curiosity of the people waiting outside the prison had been aroused by the fact that the bell had not been tolled in the customary manner, and when the prison official who posted the notice was questioned, he replied that this was quite an optional procedure.

Gill, a 26-year-old motor trolley driver, of Keighley, Yorkshire, was sentenced to death on December 13 for the murder of Oliver Preston, a Keighley moneylender.

His appeal against his conviction failed, and the Home Secretary intimated two days ago that he saw no grounds for recommending a reprieve.

WAR FILM WITHOUT MEN.

New York, Wednesday. — Although it is about war, a film which is being produced at Hollywood will have no men in it.

"Women Like Men," as it is called, will deal with the experiences of nine girls in the ambulance corps during the war.

The entire cast is of women and the directors say not even man's face will be seen, or a male voice heard. — Central News.

NO STAIN ON HIS CHARACTER.

Wrong Coat Taken by Mistake.

Two overcoats were held back to-day at the Pontypridd Police Court for the inspection of the Bench.

Allen James Dummer, a youth, of Llewellyn-street, Ynysybwl, was charged with stealing an overcoat.

The evidence of Sergeant Stockford and other witnesses was that the coat was missing from the Glyntaff School, following a social, but another coat was found in its place.

A pay ticket in an inside pocket enabled the sergeant to trace the missing coat to the possession of Dummer, who had attended the social.

It was stated that the room from which the coat was taken was in darkness, and the Bench, after inspecting the coats, and making a comparison between them, decided to accept Dummer's explanation that he took the wrong coat by mistake.

He stated that he intended to return it at the next social at the school the following week.

The Stipendiary Magistrate (Mr. D.

Gill fought for his life on the gallows, as that day's newspapers reported. (T.J. Leech Archive)

spending freely whilst on holiday and he had also paid his landlady the rent arrears prior to going away. When the police caught up with him he had £16 in cash on his person and clothes and shoes showed traces of blood on them.

Arrested and charged with Oliver Preston's murder, Gill strongly denied any involvement in the incident and when challenged about his sudden change in financial fortune he said that he had been saving up and had also won some at gambling. During the trial, before Mr Justice Talbot at Leeds, the jury heard that shortly before the murder, Gill had applied to four different moneylenders in an attempt to borrow more money, but had been refused by all of them. They also heard from Sam Maloney, an acquaintance of Gill's, who had bumped into Gill and his fiancée at Keighley railway station. Maloney had mentioned jokingly to Gill that he could do with a couple of pounds to go on holiday with and Gill had given him a pound which he said had come from a private savings club. The prosecution was able to prove that he belonged to no such club.

The defence produced two witnesses to say that they had seen Oliver Preston after the time that Gill had been seen at his office but the jury were unconvinced and after a four-day trial he was found guilty of murder and sentenced to death.

On the day of Gill's execution he put up great resistance as Pierrepoint secured his wrists and he was led to the gallows, and newspapers that evening stated that the scuffle had caused the execution to be delayed by fifteen minutes.

58

'WE HAD A QUARREL...'

Thomas Riley, 28 April 1932

On Saturday 19 December 1931, 36-year-old Irish-born Thomas Riley walked into Millgarth police station Leeds, and confessed that he had murdered his landlady in Huddersfield. Detectives hurried round to the house on Kirk Vale, Lepton, and discovered the body of 53-year-old Mrs Elizabeth Castle lying on the pantry floor. Nearby was a bloodstained hammer. Riley claimed he had struck her during a quarrel in which she had called him 'an Irish bastard.'

At Leeds Assizes, on 9 March, before Mr Justice Humphreys, the court heard that Riley was a native of Wigan, Lancashire, who had moved to Huddersfield in search of work at the end of July 1931, and had met Elizabeth Castle while both were customers in the Globe Inn. They got on well and at closing time he offered to escort the older lady to her home near Kirkheaton Church. Mrs Castle had been widowed the year before and now supplemented her income as a cleaner by taking in lodgers. Riley moved in a week or so later, and within weeks they became lovers, living as man and wife.

When Riley walked into the police station in December he had said that he wished to give himself up: 'My name is Tommy Riley and I want to give myself up for murder.' Cautioned by the desk sergeant, Riley became irate and shouted, 'I'm fed up. I am telling the truth. We had a quarrel and I hit her on the head with a hammer.' He had then handed over a door key.

Newscutting relating to the murder of Elizabeth Castle at Lepton. (T.J. Leech Archive)

MURDER OF A LEPTON WIDOW

UNEMPLOYED MINER SENTENCED TO DEATH

ACCUSED'S VERSION OF TRAGIC HAPPENINGS

The trial opened before Mr. Justice Humphreys at Leeds Assizes to-day of Thomas Riley (36), described as a miner or general labourer, of Lepton. He was charged with the murder of Elisabeth Castle, of Kirk Vale, Lepton, between December 16 and December 19.

The prisoner, who is a native of Wigan, had lived at Lepton only since July last year. The dead woman was his landlady.

When the charge was read over to him, and the formal question, "What say you, Thomas Riley, guilty or not guilty?" was put to him, he replied in a firm voice "Not guilty, my lord." He then sat down between two policemen in the dock, and folding his arms listened closely to the prosecuting barrister, Mr. G H. B. Streatfeild, outlining the case against him. Riley was defended by Mr. Raymond Hinchcliffe.

Riley told the court that on to night of the murder Mrs Castle had come home carrying a jug of beer. They shared a drink together and then an argument broke out when he refused to go outside and collect some firewood. She had then insulted him, and he then reached out, picked up a hammer and struck her with it. He went to bed that night and, the following morning, he told her daughter who lived next door that Elizabeth had gone to visit a sick friend. Riley had then travelled to Leeds, the on to Bradford before returning to Leeds and giving himself up. He offered a defence of insanity, based on head injuries he had sustained during the war and which he was receiving ongoing treatment.

In his summing up, the judge referred to the murder weapon, and said that because of its weight and size only a plea of self-defence from someone wielding such a weapon would allow any verdict other than guilty of murder.

Although he had no previous convictions, in 1925 Riley had been charged with the murder of a woman and her illegitimate child, of which he was the father. He was alleged to have killed them by pushing them into a canal but the charge was dismissed due to a lack of evidence.

59

AT THE PIGGERIES

John Henry Roberts, 28 April 1932

In addition to the greengrocer's shop on Leeds Road, Bradford, 55-year-old Alfred Gill also ran a mobile grocery round on which he was occasionally assisted by John Roberts, a 23-year-old unemployed labourer from Pudsey. On the evening of 11 December 1931, Gill failed to return home from work and a check on his movements revealed that at 5 p.m. he was seen at the gate of the piggeries he owned at Tyersal, near Pudsey. In the early hours of the following morning members of his family searched the piggeries and discovered Gill's body: he had been battered to death and dumped behind some rubbish.

John Roberts was interviewed at his lodgings in the early hours. Asked first to explain the swollen left eye he was sporting, he claimed he had bumped his head on the shaft of the grocery cart. Checking Roberts' movements of the previous night, it was discovered that at 6.30 p.m., Roberts had been in possession of one of Gill's horses, and later that night he was drinking in the Ring O'Bells pub with his girlfriend where he had paid for drinks with a 10s note.

Roberts was known to have financial problems. That summer a court judgement for debt had been made against him, for the sum of 2s a week, and as he was short of money he had so far not made any payments. Roberts was taken in and charged with murder. A search of his clothes discovered a roll of banknotes held together with a band made from a tyre inner tube exactly how Alfred Gill kept his money. When police examined the clothes Roberts had worn on the day of the murder they found them heavily bloodstained.

At Leeds Assizes on 11 March 1932 Roberts claimed that he had killed Alfred after being provoked. While they were at the piggeries, Roberts had accidentally spilled some of the food Gill was giving to his pigs. Gill swore at Roberts who had then struck him. In retaliation, Gill picked up a hammer and hit Roberts. A fight ensued and when Gill fell to the ground Roberts picked up a brick and battered him repeatedly. Roberts' watch recovered from his body was broken and at stopped at 6.13 p.m.

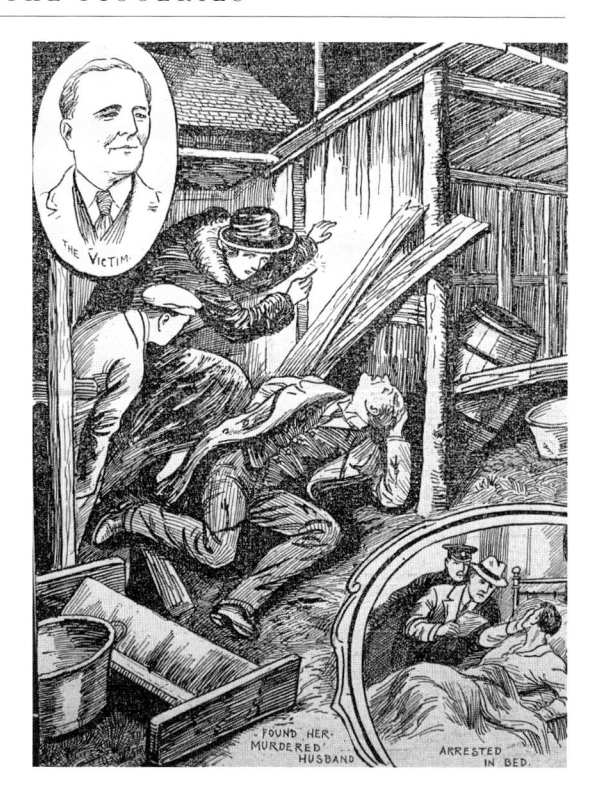

Alfred Gill's murder as sketched in the Illustrated Police News. *(T.J. Leech Archive)*

The last double execution at Leeds made front page of the Illustrated Police News. *(T.J. Leech Archive)*

Roberts offered a plea of self-defence, claiming he had been attacked first, but this was unproven and the prosecution suggested the likely motive for the crime was robbery for the killer had then stolen over £40. Following conviction, Roberts was hanged alongside Thomas Riley (*see* Chapter 58).

60

A REIGN OF TERROR

Ernest Brown, 6 February 1934

On Tuesday 5 September 1933, 28-year-old Frederick Ellison Morton, a wealthy cattle merchant, went out for the day, leaving his wife at their home at Saxton Grange, a remote farmhouse at Towton, midway between Leeds and York. Also at the farm were 35-year-old odd-job man Ernest Brown, and a nursemaid for the Morton's young child.

Earlier that summer, Morton had suspected his wife had slept with Brown, then working as a groom at the farm, and when the two men argued, Brown, in a temper, quit his job. He returned a few days later asking to be reinstated, and although Morton did take him back, it was now only as a lesser paid odd-job man. Brown was enraged and this showed in his casual approach to his work. This resulted in the farm bailiff asking Morton to dismiss him. Morton, for whatever reason, refused. It was to prove a fatal decision.

Brown had indeed been having an affair with Morton's wife, Dorothy, but their relationship was fraught with fits of violence and quarrels, and, since she had ended it, had refused his requests to rekindle the affair. That Tuesday, with Morton away for the day, Brown began drinking heavily and leaving the Boot and Shoe Inn at 8.45 p.m. he said he was going to Saxton Grange and pick up one of Morton's cars and drive to Leeds. When Brown arrived at the farm, Dorothy Morton tried to prevent him taking one of the cars. Brown lashed out at Dorothy and as she fled inside the house, he followed and collected a shotgun from one of the rooms.

Frederick Morton. (T.J. Leech Archive)

A REIGN OF TERROR

Morton's body was discovered in a burnt-out car at Saxton Grange. (TNA PRO)

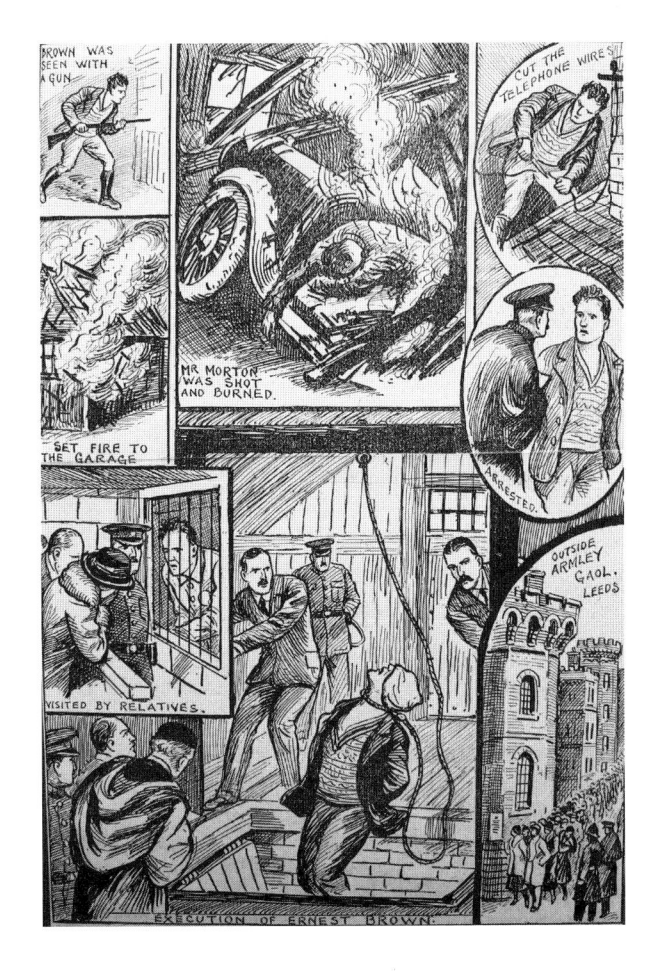

The Illustrated Police News *recalls the Saxton Grange murder. (T.J. Leech Archive)*

95

Ernest Brown. Did he confess to another murder on the scaffold? (T.J. Leech Archive)

Newscutting relating to the Saxton Grange murder. (T.J. Leech Archive)

Over the next few hours, Brown set about a frightening campaign: terrorising Dorothy, her young daughter and the nursemaid, cutting the telephone wires and firing a shotgun at the house as Mrs Morton and her housekeeper sat terrified behind the locked door.

Finally, at 3.30 a.m. the following morning, a dull explosion was heard and looking through the window, Dorothy saw that the garage was on fire. The police and the fire brigade arrived at the farm and when the fire was put out and cars examined, inside one was the body of Frederick Morton. He had been shot dead.

Brown was arrested on 7 September and brought before Mr Justice Humphreys in December. It was found that Morton had been killed at approximately 9 p.m. that Tuesday night, shortly after Brown had returned from the pub and before he had began his reign of terror at the house.

Brown simply denied the charge of murder and, as it had been shown in court that Dorothy Morton had had several lovers, he suggested another of Dorothy's beaus might have carried it out. After a three-day trial at Leeds Assizes, he was convicted after a twenty-minute deliberation by the jury and sentenced to death. A petition containing over 10,000 signatures was sent to the Home Office, and enquiries were made into Brown's state of mind.

On the eve of his execution, Brown made an extraordinary confession that Mrs Morton had killed her husband and that he lied to protect her. A last minute conference with the Lord Chief Justice failed to prevent the law taking its course and Brown went to gallows as planned. But there was still one more twist.

With Brown noosed and on the scaffold he made one brief remark as the hangman went to push the lever: 'Ought to burn', or was it 'Otterburn'? Pierrepoint was unsure of the exact words, but if it had been 'Otterburn' it may have been a confession to another murder.

On Tuesday 6 January 1931, taxi driver Evelyn Foster, who worked for her father's company, picked up a fare in Otterburn, Northumberland. The man asked to be taken to Ponteland, but midway through the journey he changed his mind and asked to go back to Otterburn. When questioned why, she claimed he punched her in the face before pouring petrol over her and the taxi and setting it alight. Evelyn Foster died from her extensive injuries the following day. However, it seems the police were sceptical of her claims and investigating officers suspected that she had been fatally injured whilst setting fire to the taxi to defraud the insurance company. As a result the case was not fully investigated and never solved. Perhaps Evelyn Foster had been telling the truth after all?

61

THE BOXING DAY MURDER

Lewis Hamilton, 6 April 1934

A few days before Christmas 1933, 25-year-old Lewis Hamilton, a butcher's assistant and slaughter man from Bradford, received a summons to go to court regarding a separation order taken out by his wife, Maud. Hamilton and his wife had married in July of that year and a short time later she gave birth to their first child. They were living at his mother's house when, in December, they parted after a quarrel and she went back to her own mother's at 39 Jermyn Street, Stott Hill, Bradford.

Hamilton had a fiery temper and on 23 December a visit to see his wife ended with him swearing, kicking and assaulting her. On the following day Maud reported Hamilton to the police and he was duly served with a summons for assault. Handed the summons, Hamilton simply replied, 'Well, she's been asking for it!'

Three days later, Hamilton again went to see his wife. Reaching the house he banged on the door and shouted, 'Open the door, I have something to show you.' Fearing trouble, Hamilton was refused entry and left without seeing his wife. Instead he called on his brother-in-law and showed him the summons, and while there he picked up a large butcher's knife.

Hamilton returned to Jermyn Street and waited for his wife to appear. By now he knew she was in the house of a neighbour and at 4 p.m., as Maud made her way home, Hamilton grabbed her and dragged her into her mother's house. A crowd, alerted by the shouting in the street, gathered, and eventually a man broke the door down as screams rang out. Inside, Hamilton held the bloodstained knife in his hand: Maud Hamilton lay on the floor, her throat cut.

Hamilton was almost lynched by neighbours and needed to be rescued by police officers, to whom he immediately admitted the attack. 'I quite realise what I have done. Take me back to see,' Hamilton said, before being charged with murder.

He offered a defence of epilepsy and insanity at his trial at West Riding Assizes, Leeds, on 15 March 1934. There, no medical evidence could be found to suggest insanity, other than the fact Hamilton's father had died from epilepsy in 1914, and that the officer who had arrested Hamilton at the scene claimed that the prisoner seemed dazed when taken into custody.

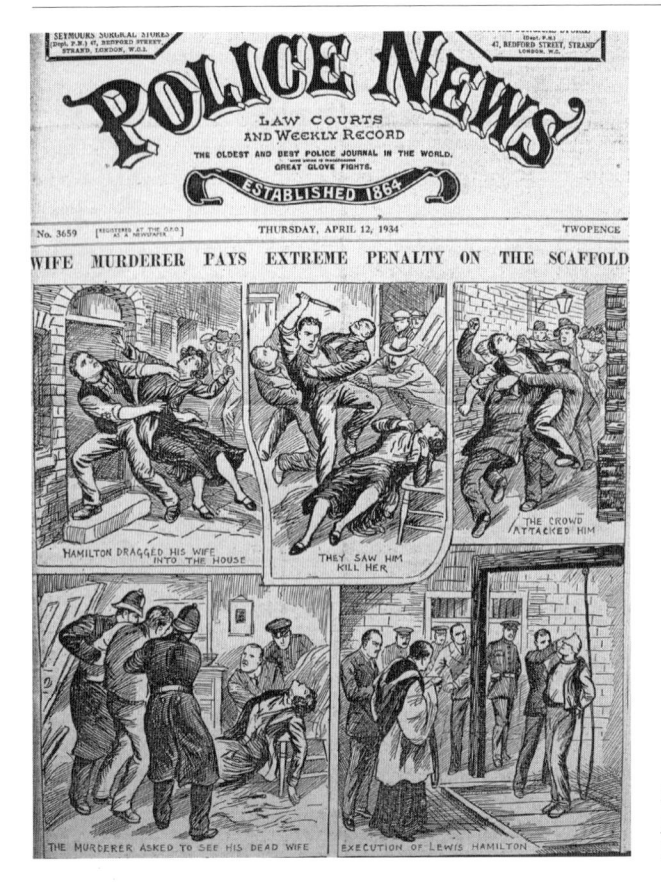

Hamilton's execution made the front page of the Illustrated Police News. *(T.J. Leech Archive)*

Dr Francis Brisby, Medical Officer at Leeds Prison, told the court he had had Hamilton under observation since the beginning of January and there was nothing in his behaviour to suggest that Hamilton was insane. The jury agreed and it was left to Mr Commissioner H.H. Joy KC to sentence him to death. The jury added a strong recommendation for mercy but an appeal failed, as did a petition with over 30,000 signatures presented to the Lord Mayor of Bradford.

62

PUT AWAY QUIETLY

Frederick Rushworth, 1 January 1935

Fred Rushworth, a 29-year-old farm labourer from Gellpool, near Middleham, and 24-year-old Lydia Binks, had been living together since the summer of 1932. Although a mother of two young children, Lydia was childlike in thoughts and manner and regarded locally as 'a bit simple'.

They moved in together and in the summer of 1933 she again found herself pregnant. In January 1934, although by now seven months pregnant, Lydia took a job working at a holiday camp near Wensleydale, a camp that contained both caravans and chalets.

On 1 March, Lydia gave birth to a daughter, somehow managing to conceal the confinement from the camp owner. However, when he heard the baby crying and went to investigate, Lydia told him she was looking after it for a friend who was in hospital. The owner told her he did not want a crying child disturbing holidaymakers and she would have to return it to the mother.

On 25 March Lydia met Rushworth at Wensley Bridge and told him that it would be best if the child were placed with a nurse. Rushworth said they couldn't afford to do this and suggested the child should be 'put away quietly'. She refused to go along with this and claimed later that as they walked through a field, Rushworth snatched the child and buried it alive in a hole he had dug with a spade.

Without the burden of the child, Lydia was able to continue working and it was several months until the matter came to the attention of the police. They questioned Lydia about the baby's whereabouts and she made no attempt to disguise what had happened, taking officers to the woods where she had gone with Rushworth and pointing to the spot she believed the baby had been buried. There, in a shallow grave, was the baby's body and tests later found that it had been alive when placed in the ground.

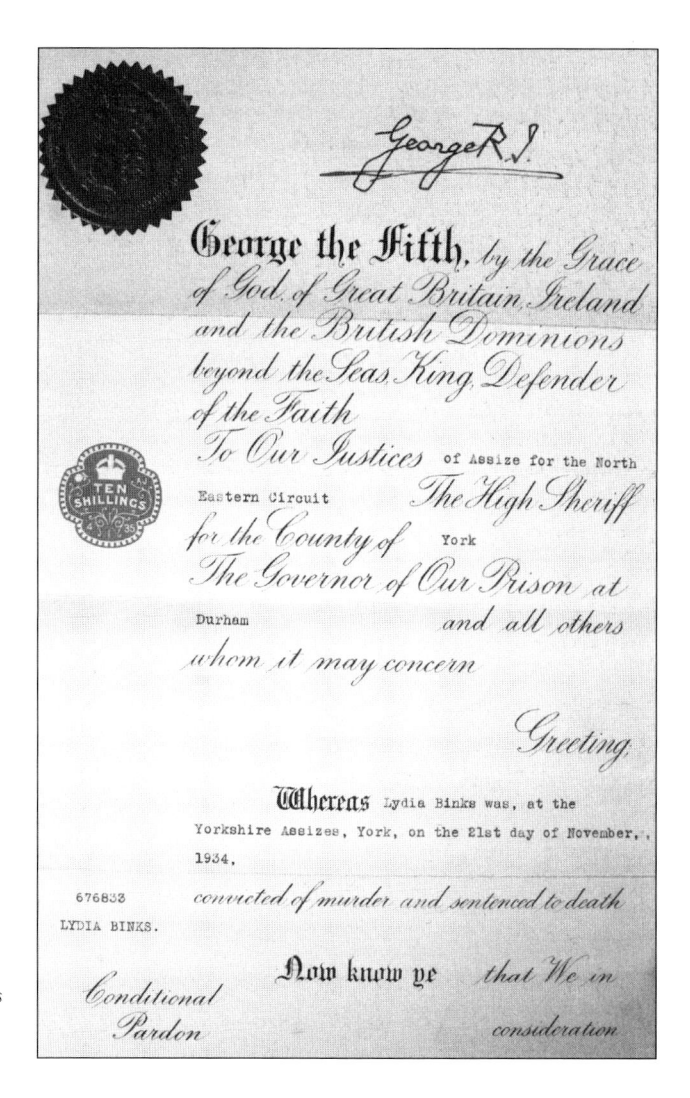

Official Royal Pardon of Lydia Binks signed by King George. (Author's collection)

Rushworth and Binks were jointly charged with murder, and at their trial at York before Mr Justice Porter on 21 November, Lydia claimed that Rushworth had told her they could not afford a nurse for the child and they would 'put it away quietly'. She said Rushworth had then dug the hole, placed the child still in its basket into the hole, and covered it with earth.

Rushworth told a different story. He claimed that the child had been quiet and unmoving and he believed Lydia had brought it to him because it was dead, and all he had done was bury the child. On the second day of the trial, both defendants were found guilty and sentenced to death. The jury believed the prosecution's case that both were equally guilty, although there was no doubt Rushworth had used his influence over Binks to get her to go along with the scheme to remove the burden of the child.

They were due to hang on the same date, 13 December 1934, but at different prisons. Rushworth was taken to Armley while Lydia Binks was sent to Durham Gaol. They appealed against their convictions and Binks' counsel cited the Infanticide Act of 1922, which outlawed the death penalty for mothers of newborn babies. Dismissing this claim, the appeal judges pointed out that the Act related to newly born children, whilst in this case the un-named child was over three weeks old and outside the scope of the Act.

New execution dates of 1 January 1935 were set. Binks returned to Durham, where, two days before she was to face the hangman, she was reprieved. For Frederick Rushworth there would be no such mercy.

63

A TERRIBLE SECRET

David Maskill Blake, 7 February 1935

It was early on the morning of Wednesday 17 October 1934 when a man walking through Middleton Woods, Leeds, stumbled across the body of a young woman. Lying face down in bracken, she had been strangled by a pink scarf wrapped around her neck and from the state of her clothes it seems her killer had attempted a sexual assault.

Identified as Emily Yeomans, a 23-year-old waitress at Lyons Café in the County Arcade, detectives soon mounted a huge search, even bringing in bloodhounds in the hunt for clues. A large reward for

Emily Yeomans. (T.J. Leech Archive)

Rapist and strangler David Blake committed murder the day before he was married. (T.J. Leech Archive)

information was also offered to help catch the killer. Officers learned that Emily lived with her uncle in the Dewsbury Road area of the city, and he told detectives that on the previous evening Emily had left home to meet a man, but he told officers he did not know the man's name nor would he be able to identify him.

Enquiries among Emily's friends soon led police to make an arrest. Joseph Talbot was picked up and interrogated when forensic evidence linked him to the dead girl. Talbot admitted he had taken her out on more than one occasion, and police believed they had their man when Talbot was identified by one of the boys who had seen Emily in the company of a the man on the evening before she was found dead. The evidence against him, however, was too weak to hold him, and with nothing further linking him to the murder he was released.

Officers didn't have to wait long to make another arrest. Eight days later David Blake, a 29-year-old unemployed steel erector, of Lady Pit Lane, Leeds, was detained. Blake had been married on the same morning that Emily's body was discovered, and his behaviour since had aroused suspicion. Word reached detectives that he may be linked with the murder and when questioned, officers found hairs on his clothes that matched those of Emily's cat. Also discovered was a damaged face-powder compact that belonged to Miss Yeomans, and which was discovered at a house where Blake had stayed after the murder.

Blake stood trial before Mr Justice Goddard at Leeds Assizes on 12 December. It was to last three days. Blake's best man at his wedding told the court that he and Blake had been out drinking during the afternoon of 15 October, and at about 9.40 p.m. the two men had parted on Dewsbury Road and he saw Blake meet a girl he recognised as Emily Yeomans.

Another witness said that on the evening of 17 October he met Blake, who seemed nervous and talked non-stop about the murder, even asking to see a copy of the *Evening Post*. Blake later took a compact from his pocket and offered it to him. Three waitresses who worked with Emily Yeomans identified it by the damaged lid.

Blake could offer no defence to the charges other than a denial, and it took the jury just seventy-five minutes to reach their verdict. Passing sentence of death, Mr Justice Goddard told Blake, 'You have been found guilty of as cruel, treacherous and brutal a murder as in many years experience of the law I have come across.'

Following conviction, it was revealed that Blake had a history of rape. In March 1930 he had been sentenced to three years for an attack on a servant girl after offering to walk her home when she had missed her bus, and he had previously served two years for rape while serving with the army in India.

64

HIS GIRL

Andrew Anderson Bagley, 10 February 1937

In October 1932, Andrew Bagley's common-law wife died, leaving him with numerous debts. He refused to pay her creditors and instead chose to move around the country using names such as Anderson and John Smith. In August 1936 he moved in with his daughter and son-in-law, Mr and Mrs Hart, in Rotherham, and still fearful of creditors, he would hide in an upstairs cupboard whenever anyone called.

Also living in the small two-up two-down terraced house on Hartington Road was Bagley's mentally ill son, Ambrose, and the Hart's 16-year-old daughter, Irene. On 29 August, Irene went to the pictures with one of her uncles and another man. On their return, Bagley made a dreadful scene. He shouted at Irene that it was not right for one girl to go out with two men, adding that Irene was 'his girl' and no one else's. This was not the first time Bagley referred to Irene as his girl, but nobody seemed to make anything of it.

On Saturday morning, 12 September, Mrs Hart left the house, leaving Bagley and Irene in the kitchen. She returned at 11.15 a.m. and found Bagley alone, wearing his overcoat. She asked where Irene was and Bagley replied that he had given her a pound note and sent her to the Cosy Corner Shop and she had not returned. He then added that he was going to Sheffield.

When Irene failed to return, her father went to inform the police, and while he was there Mrs Hart noticed that the attic trapdoor was open. She climbed up and found Irene's dress, gloves and handbag, alongside toys normally kept in a tin trunk under Irene's bed. She opened the trunk and discovered the body of her daughter. Irene had been strangled with a rope, which was tied once around her neck. Newspaper was stuffed in her mouth, her dress was torn and her underclothes were missing. A pathologist confirmed intercourse had taken place shortly before her death.

As a nationwide hunt began, Bagley made his way to Liverpool, where he took lodgings in the name of Arthur Wilson. He stayed there until 6 October before moving to Manchester, then finally to Hucknall near Nottingham, where he was arrested.

At Leeds Assizes before Mr Justice Goddard, Bagley pleaded not guilty. Bagley claimed that Irene had been with a man named Tom on the morning of her death and that this man must be the killer. There was no evidence of anyone called Tom, despite Bagley's claim that she had shown him a letter written by Tom. Irene's

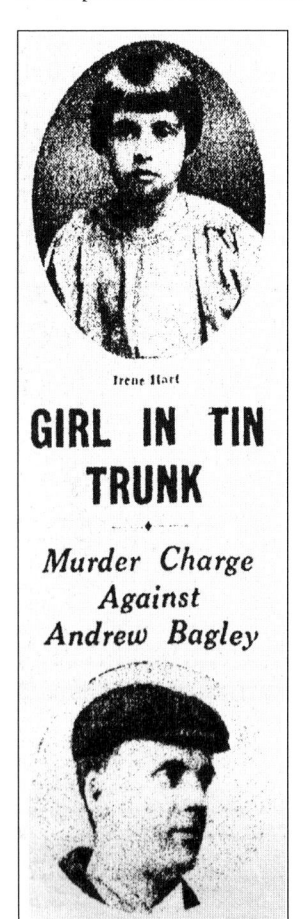

Irene Hart and Andrew Bagley pictured in the newspapers. (T.J. Leech Archive)

How the Illustrated Police News *recorded the execution of Andrew Bagley. (T.J. Leech Archive)*

father told the court that Bagley had become very fond of Irene during his stay and due to the lack of space in the house Bagley slept on the floor in Irene's room.

Summing up, Mr Justice Goddard said the case was extraordinary only in the disparity of age between Irene and Bagley. According to the Crown, said the judge, the only people in the house on 12 September were Irene, Bagley and his mentally ill son, Ambrose. This discounted the son: he had the strength and mind of a child of 6 and could not have tied the knot in the rope that strangled the girl.

During the summing up a member of the jury was taken ill, and it was agreed that the verdict could be decided by the remaining eleven. It took the remaining members just thirty minutes to reach a verdict of guilty as charged.

65

DEATH AT THE FAIRGROUND

Trevor Elvin, 10 September 1943

On the morning of Tuesday 4 May 1943, a young woman was discovered with severe head injuries beside the dodgem-car tent at a fairground on the outskirts of Barnsley. She was rushed to the local hospital while detectives began a hunt for her attacker. A broken, rusty hammer was discovered close by and although at this stage they were only dealing with a case of attempted murder, officers in Barnsley immediately called in the assistance of Scotland Yard. Detective Chief Inspector Peter Beveridge arrived to take over the investigation, and on arriving in the town he learned that the woman, who had never regained consciousness, had since died from her injuries.

The victim was 20-year-old Violet Wakefield of Cudworth. Violet was a member of the Woman's Land Army, who worked as a lorry driver's assistant, and investigations soon led to her former boyfriend, Trevor Elvin, a 21-year-old glass worker living with his parents on Grove Street, Barnsley. The couple had been courting for two years, and although they had discussed marriage, his father did not think them old enough. Elvin and Violet had recently quarrelled after he accused her of being too familiar with the lorry driver she worked with, and on the previous weekend she had broken off their engagement.

Witnesses said that shortly before the body was discovered, Violet was seen walking towards the fairground in the company of a man. Detectives went to Elvin's home and discovered he had gone to visit relatives in Blackpool. Questioned about the murder, Elvin told the police that Miss Wakefield and he had had an argument over a man named Bob, but he had been in Blackpool since the previous day so could not be the man seen in her company shortly before she died.

When shown the hammer found at the scene of the murder, Elvin denied having seen it before, but a search at his home had discovered a broken piece of flat hammerhead, which fitted the missing piece from the suspected murder weapon perfectly. Also found in his room was a diary in which he had written: 'I am sure Violet is in love with Bob, but he will never win her. I am not jealous of Violet; but she has changed.'

Charged with wilful murder, Elvin stood trial before Mr Justice Tucker at Leeds Assizes on 12 July, and pleaded guilty but insane. The prosecution alleged that the motive was unfounded jealousy, and there was no sign of insanity, claiming that Elvin had told police that he had a hammer in his raincoat pocket but that he had only meant to frighten her.

66

THE VITAL CLUE

Mervin Clare McEwen, 3 February 1944

On Saturday afternoon, 3 April 1943, the body of 82-year-old Mark Turner was discovered in his end-terrace house at Moorfield Street, Halifax. For over forty years the old man had worked as a postman in and around Halifax, before retiring in March 1922. His battered body was discovered when neighbours, concerned for his whereabouts, had contacted the police. A police constable found the old man's body in a folding settee bed: he had been battered around the head with a hammer. Missing from the house where ration books, an identity card and items of jewellery, but the killer had left a vital clue.

Beside the body was an army tunic with the number A29600 written inside. This was traced to a private in the Canadian Ordnance Corp, 35-year-old Mervin McEwen. McEwen was a tall half-Scot half-Canadian, with a distinctive Scottish accent, who had absconded from his unit in the south of England two months earlier. Turner's friends and neighbours told police that the solider had been living rough in Saville Park, Halifax for several days prior to the murder and that the old man had, on more than one occasion, offered him a room and refreshments at his house.

McEwen was finally picked up in Manchester and when taken into custody was found to be in possession of ration and identity cards belonging to Mark Turner. He admitted he had broken into the old man's house while cold and hungry with the intention of stealing some food. While he was in the house Turner had woken up and he had picked up the hammer to stop the old man from crying out. He then picked up a knife and had stabbed him through the bedclothes to 'shut him up'.

Before Mr Justice Stable at Leeds Assizes in December, McEwen admitted that he had hit him once but had no recollection of carrying out any further attacks. His defence counsel claimed that McEwen was so incapacitated with drink he was incapable of forming the necessary intention to commit murder, and that the correct verdict in this case was manslaughter.

Mark Turner. (T.J. Leech Archive)

SCOTLAND YARD CALLED IN HALIFAX MURDER INVESTIGATIONS

Hunt For Scots Canadian With Dead Man's Property

A brutal murder was discovered by Halifax Borough Police on Saturday afternoon. The victim was Mr. Mark Turner, widower, and retired postman, aged 82, of 1, Moorfield-street, in the Emscote district.

The co-operation of Scotland Yard has been secured in the investigations.

IN BED SETTEE.

Mr. Turner, who had good health in spite of his age, was usually about, but as he had not been seen on Saturday, neighbours informed the police. Upon entering the house the police found the body of Mr. Turner in a settee folding bed. His head was battered in. The evidences pointed to death having taken place a considerable time

Newscutting announces that Scotland Yard are called in to investigate the murder of Mark Turner. (T.J. Leech Archive)

Mervin Clare McEwen. (T.J. Leech Archive)

Mr Justice Stable told the jury that if they believed the accused's version of events, manslaughter was not an option, and they must then return a verdict of wilful murder, which they did.

67

THE KILLER WITH BLOOD GROUP 'A'

Arthur Thompson, 31 January 1945

On the morning of Thursday 21 September 1944, a neighbour, alerted by the sound of a dog barking, discovered a broken window at the rear of the Nags Head public house at Clayton Heights, Bradford. On closer inspection she found a glass panel in the back door had also been smashed and she hurried to call the police.

PC Frank Thorpe was first to the scene. Finding the back door unlocked, he entered the premises, shouting for the landlady, 69-year-old Jane Coulton, as he walked from room to room. Venturing upstairs, he discovered her body lying in her bed, a stocking tied tightly around her neck.

The Nags Head at Bradford, where Arthur Thompson committed murder. (T.J. Leech Archive)

A post-mortem found that the old lady had been punched in the head before being strangled. It was also clear that during the murderous attack the killer had shed blood at the scene of the crime, as there was blood from both Group B, found to belong to Jane Coulton, and Group A, presumably belonging to the killer. It seemed clear that robbery was the motive as missing from the pub was a quantity of money, along with some of the dead woman's jewellery.

Investigations into likely suspects soon turned up the name of Arthur Thompson, a 34-year-old Liverpudlian lance corporal in the General Service Corp, stationed nearby. Thompson had been hospitalised following a street brawl and had been released on the previous Monday, but had been AWOL since the night of the murder. Thompson had been a regular at the Nags Head in recent times and detectives learned that on the night before the murder he had told a friend that he was short of money and intended breaking in somewhere to get some. It was also discovered that on the morning following the murder, Thompson had visited friends and settled a number of debts.

The hunt for Thompson was brief. On 23 September, a soldier, identified as Thompson, sold a watch to a jeweller in Heysham, near Morecambe, and the following day tried to sell a woman's ring to George Slater, the licensee of the Globe Hotel at Overton. Slater's suspicions were aroused and he called the police. Thompson was arrested as he tried to flee the premises.

On the way to the police station, Thompson asked if they would stop the car, as he needed to use the toilet. Told they would soon be at the station, his request was refused. Sergeant Sidney Wood drove the car to the station, which was not used again that day. The following morning, as Wood cleaned the car, he noticed one of the mats had been moved. Lifting it, he discovered a small parcel containing items of jewellery that belonged to Jane Coulton. Thompson's hands had small cuts on them and under close examination his battledress was stained with his own blood: Group A.

Charged with murder, Thompson appeared in due course before Mr Justice Oliver at Leeds Assizes. Although he blamed the murder on a man named Buck, no trace of the mystery man could be found. The evidence against Thompson was strong; not withstanding the matching bloodstains found at the public house, the jewellery belonging the dead woman found in the police car, which could only have been placed there by the prisoner, was enough for the jury to convict him.

Newscutting announces another Bradford murder. (T.J. Leech Archive)

68

THROUGH JEALOUSY

Thomas Eric Richardson, 7 September 1945

In the early hours of Sunday morning, 29 April 1945, the body of David Walker Dewar, a 41-year-old Scottish-born doctor, was found lying in the driveway at his home on Beeston Road, Leeds. He had been battered about the head with a sharp weapon, seemingly as he had been opening the garage door.

Police officers soon discovered that behind the façade of respectability, the doctor, though popular and well regarded by his patients, was a heavy-drinking womaniser with a string of mistresses across the city. Among these women was Laura Walker, the wife of a soldier serving overseas. When questioned, she told detectives she had first met David Dewar long before her marriage and that he had been the family doctor since 1931. Following her marriage she had begun an affair with him and this had continued while her husband was serving overseas.

The body of Dr Dewar outside his home in Leeds. (TNA PRO)

Detectives also learned that Dr Dewar wasn't the only man Laura Walker was seeing behind her husband's back. Thomas Eric Richardson, a 27-year-old local engineer, had been a close friend of Laura's husband, but he too had begun a clandestine relationship with her. On the night before the murder Laura had confessed to Richardson of her relationship with Dr Dewar, and that she was meeting him that night. Richardson seemed upset, but accepted the situation when she told him she had no plans to end the affair with the doctor.

Following Dewar's murder, Laura Walker spoke to Richardson about it, but although he initially denied any involvement, once the police began to ask questions he confessed to her that he had killed Dr Dewar. Following his arrest, Richardson said that he had been drinking and could recall little of what had happened between leaving the Hope Inn until he finally arrived at Laura's house in the early hours. Under questioning, Richardson admitted that he had killed the doctor with an axe in a jealous rage, and had then thrown the murder weapon into a nearby river.

Dr Dewar. (T.J. Leech Archive)

At his trial before Mr Justice Hallett at Leeds in July, Richardson initially denied making any confessions, but also offered a defence of insanity. His counsel claimed that Richardson had killed Dewar during a temporary blackout caused by epilepsy. Believing the prosecution's claims that this was a brutal murder caused through jealousy, the jury returned a guilty verdict, added a strong recommendation to mercy. His appeal was dismissed with the panel claiming it was brutal, premeditated murder with no extenuating circumstance sufficient to justify a reprieve.

69

HOME FROM THE WAR

William Batty, 8 January 1946

On 10 August 1945, soldier's wife Nellie Grey received a telegram at her home on Prince Street, Dudley Hill, Bradford, informing her that her husband, 33-year-old Samuel Grey, would be arriving home the following day. Grey had been serving in Burma but had posted the telegram when his ship landed in England.

Unbeknown to Grey, for the last three years his wife had been having a relationship with 27-year-old William Batty, a single man who lived close by with his mother. When Batty heard of the return he said he would speak to Grey, and tell him to stay away from Nellie or he would shoot him.

A day after Grey returned home, Batty wrote a letter to Nellie asking her to run away with him. Not only did she refuse his request, but she also showed it to her husband and claimed that Batty had

The body of Samuel Grey lies in the hallway at his home following his shooting by William Batty. (TNA PRO)

A letter informing Harry Allen of details regarding William Batty's execution. (Author's collection)

Details of Batty's execution in Harry Allen's diary. (Author's collection)

been making unwanted advances to her. On Tuesday evening, 14 August, there was a knock on the door at the house on Prince Street. Grey answered the door and found himself face to face with Batty, who asked to speak to Nellie. Asked his name, Batty replied, 'I am nobody!' He then pulled out a Luger pistol and fired a single shot. As Samuel Grey fell dead in the hallway, Batty hurried back to his mother's, where he was arrested a short while later.

Batty was a habitual criminal with a number of convictions for larceny, and had served three years imprisonment shortly before he became involved with Mrs Grey. At his trial before Mr Justice Lynskey at Leeds that November, he claimed that after he had gone to the house to discuss the situation, Grey had pulled out a gun on him, which had gone off accidentally during a struggle. This was refuted by witnesses who saw him toying with a gun outside the house prior to the murder, and he was duly convicted.

70

THE MOST SORDID OF MOTIVES

Albert Sabin, 30 January 1947

On Saturday afternoon, 21 September 1946, the body of Dr Neil McLeod, a 52-year-old Leeds-based psychiatrist, was found in a ditch in the grounds of Topcliffe Pit, a disused colliery on the outskirts of the city, close to a POW camp at Tingley Hall. He had been shot dead.

McLeod was one of the leading mental-health specialists in the north of England; with a thriving practice in Park Square, Leeds. As the body had been found close to the army camp, detectives routinely questioned personnel stationed at the camp and soon learned that Dr McLeod had been seen a few hours before his body was discovered giving a soldier a lift in his car. Passing through the gates at Tingley Hall, they noticed the doctor's Ford V8 in the camp compound, which they learned was being driven by one of the guards, 21-year-old Albert Sabin. Sabin had told his superiors previously that he was going into Leeds to collect a car he had been given by a relative, and had returned with the Ford. Under questioning, he immediately confessed that he had killed the doctor, but claimed it was an accident.

The entrance to Topcliffe Pit, where the body of Dr McLeod was discovered. (TNA PRO)

Albert Sabin. (T.J. Leech Archive)

Albert Sabin was the first of fifteen men hanged at Leeds by Steve Wade. (Author's collection)

Trail led to Crime Doctor

DR. NEIL MCLEOD, one of the leading psychiatrists in the North of England, believed that many criminals were not responsible for their crimes.

He attended his patients in Leeds as usual on Saturday. His wife expected him to return for his afternoon spell of gardening—his only hobby.

But he never arrived.

She inquired for him at Leeds Infimary. Meanwhile, the police were following a trail of blood found by a youth at a disused Morley colliery, several miles from the doctor's home.

Along the trail they saw a tobacco pouch, a penknife, two handkerchiefs, a box

Dr. McLeod

Newscutting relating to the murder of Dr McLeod. (T.J. Leech Archive)

Birmingham-born Sabin was taken to Morley police station, where he claimed that McLeod had made improper advances to him and the gun had accidentally gone off during a struggle in the car. Sabin claimed that he had recently got to know Dr MacLeod and the doctor had given him a lift back to camp on a number of occasions. He said that on that Saturday afternoon he had gone to the doctor's surgery with the intention of borrowing some money from MacLeod. Sabin said he had taken a gun with him and claimed that he only recalled firing once, but he had taken some money before dragging McLeod's body to the ditch and driving off in his car.

At his trial before Mr Justice Henn-Collins in December, the defence claimed that Sabin had killed Dr MacLeod after the doctor had tried to sexually assault him. Sabin said that on the afternoon of the murder the doctor had promised him a lift back to the camp but instead he had turned off down the pit road, claiming that he had a call to make. MacLeod then tried to kiss him and as Sabin climbed out of the car, he claimed that MacLeod attempted to pull him back in and the gun went off accidentally.

The prosecution disputed this: rather than one shot, as Sabin claimed, a post-mortem had found three bullet wounds: one in the chest, one in the neck and one in the head. They also suggested a motive: Sabin had been trying to blackmail the doctor and after shooting him he had stolen money to the value of £20.

Following conviction, Sabin's appeal in January 1947 was quickly dismissed, with the Lord Chief Justice claiming that it was a clear case of murder with the most sordid of motives – robbery. Unless it had been under duress, they could find no logical reason why Dr McLeod should turn into the grounds of a disused pit in the company of a soldier, but they disputed any allegations made by Sabin as to Dr McLeod making sexual advances and refused Sabin's request to call further evidence to support this claim.

71

WITNESS FOR THE PROSECUTION

Eric Charles Briggs, 20 June 1947

The hardest task for detectives investigating the murder of Gertrude Briggs at Leeds was deciding which of the two suspects, who had both confessed to the crime, was telling the truth. Eric Briggs and his wife Gertrude lived on Caledonian Road, Leeds. Forty-year-old Briggs had carried out many and varied types of employment, although he was often unemployed for long periods of time, while 49-year-old Gertrude was employed as a kitchen maid in a Leeds Hotel.

In the early hours of 10 February 1947, Gertrude left work having finished her shift and headed home. Later that morning her body was discovered on a deserted side street. She had been stabbed to death, with nearly fifty wounds to her neck and body. It was the second brutal attack on a woman in the city recently; a week earlier Elizabeth Donoghue received a fractured skull and severe cuts to her hands and face after a late night assault. Luckily she survived her ordeal.

When police notified Briggs of his wife's death, they found bloodstains on his hands and he was immediately arrested on suspicion of the murder. After initially denying being involved, on the following night he confessed he had killed her with a hacksaw blade. At this point the case should

HANGED AT LEEDS

The street where Gertrude Briggs was murdered. (T.J. Leech Archive)

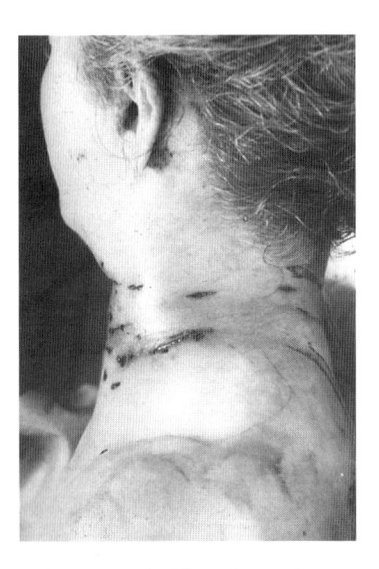

Police photograph of the neck wounds sustained by Gertrude Briggs. (TNA PRO)

Gertrude Briggs, murdered by her husband. (T.J. Leech Archive)

have been fairly straightforward. However, two days later, a soldier from Leeds was arrested in Sheffield. His name was Dennis Wood and he confessed to attacking both Mrs Donoghue and Mrs Briggs.

Despite this, Briggs' trial for the murder of his wife went ahead as planned before Mr Justice Pritchard in May. Having heard about Wood's confession to his wife's murder, Briggs had by now retracted his own confession. The prosecution produced a witness who stated that Briggs had admitted to him whilst they were in Leeds Prison awaiting trial that he had carried out the murder, and how he had sharpened the murder weapon beforehand.

The defence suggested strongly that police had 'influenced' Briggs to confess, and on the second day of the trial they produced what they believed would be their key witness. Dennis Wood took the stand to give evidence and admitted that it was he who had attacked and killed Mrs Briggs, although he said he had stabbed her with his bayonet. The prosecution contested this and called medical evidence to show that the wounds were more consistent with having been inflicted by a hacksaw blade than a bayonet. Wood's testimony was so destroyed that, rather than help the defence, he became almost a witness for the prosecution.

Eric Briggs was duly found guilty of his wife's murder and sentenced to death. The following day, Dennis Wood stood trial and was convicted of the attempted murder of Elizabeth Donoghue. He was ordered to be detained at His Majesty's Pleasure. Briggs was hanged a month later.

72

TWO MOTIVES

William Smedley, 14 August 1947

Friday 7 March 1947 broke as a cold and frosty morning. On a snow-covered building site on Bridge Street, close to Sheffield city centre, the body of a young woman was found strangled with a scarf knotted tightly around her throat. Identified as Edith Simmonite, a 29-year-old Sheffield prostitute, forensic tests revealed that she had had sex shortly before she had died. Witnesses soon told police they had seen her in the company of two men from a local hostel, one of whom was identified as 38-year-old miner William Smedley, who lived in a hostel at West Bar.

Interviewed by Murder Squad detectives, Smedley, with a long list of convictions for stealing and indecency, claimed that he and a friend had met up briefly with Edith on the night she died, but that both he and his friend had bid her goodnight outside the hostel before going inside together. A chat with the friend soon put Smedley in the frame. He disputed Smedley's version of events, instead claiming that when he went inside the hostel and upstairs to his room, Smedley was still talking to Edith at the corner of the street.

Questioned by detectives, Smedley, a known former client of the dead woman, said he had been chatting to Edith when an Irishman approached them. After a brief exchange of words, Edith went off to do business with the Irishman. Smedley said that he had since spoken to the Irishman and that he had confessed to him he had committed the murder and was going to Rhyl in North Wales.

As the investigation continued and the hunt for the mysterious Irishman drew a blank, Smedley sent a telegram to his sister asking her to 'Come Saturday morning. Urgent. Brother in terrible trouble.' Smedley's sister called to see him and he confessed to her that he had killed Edith Simmonite.

Three days later, on 13 May, Smedley was arrested and charged with murder. He made a further statement in which he now admitted that he had gone with Edith and had sex with her. As he readjusted his clothes she told him that she had venereal disease, and in a rage he had gripped the scarf around her neck and strangled her.

Edith Simmonite. (Author's collection)

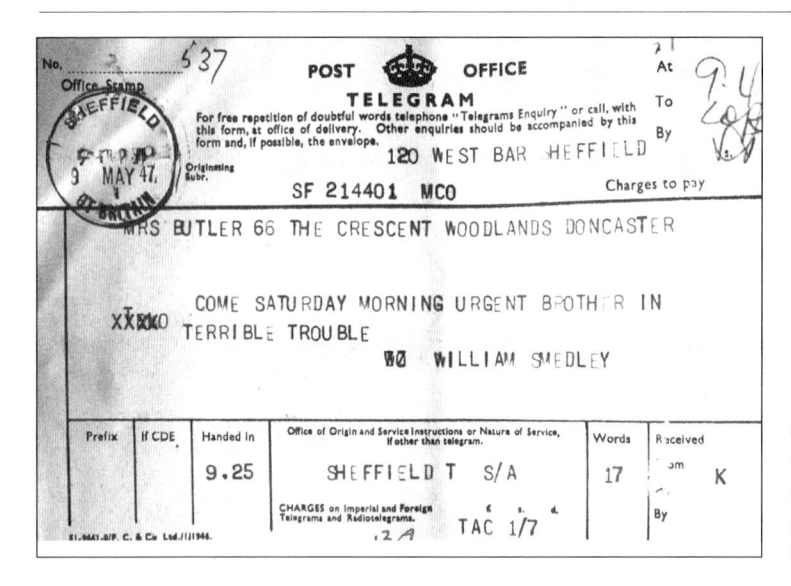

Telegram sent by William Smedley shortly before he confessed to murder. (Author's collection)

Tried before Mr Justice Pritchard at Leeds Assizes on 22 July, the prosecution suggested that Smedley had two motives for killing her. Firstly, Edith had robbed him of some money during a previous liaison, and secondly, on the night of her death, following sex she had revealed that she had infected him with a sexually transmitted disease. In a rage that he had strangled her.

Under cross-examination it was found that Smedley had already been infected with V.D. following previous liaison with Edith, and had been undergoing treatment, so there was no question of a spur-of-the-moment reaction to hearing he had been infected with the disease. Instead, this suggested a revenge killing, and the jury agreed.

73

A 'SPIV AND A WIDE-BOY'

John Edward Gartside, 21 August 1947

Percy and Alice Baker, both in their early forties, disappeared suddenly in the late spring of 1947. They had a Sunday routine with friends, Mr and Mrs Leonard Doughty, that if the Doughtys hadn't arrived at the Baker's house, at Manor House Farm, Standedge, by 2 p.m., then the Bakers would walk the mile or so down the road and lunch with their friends across the Lancashire/Yorkshire border at their home in Dobcross.

The routine had been broken on Sunday 25 May, when the Bakers failed to show for lunch and when, in the following days, Mrs Baker failed to show up for a number of engagements with friends, one of them called at the farmhouse and was shocked to find a removal van outside. The van bore the name 'Gold Lea & Co.' with an address in Oldham. The owner of the firm, Mr Libman, told her that Baker had gone into the shop on the previous Thursday and said he and his wife had separated and

Manor House Farm, Standedge. (TNA PRO)

that he wanted to sell the furniture. The friend thought this highly suspicious and notified the police, who discovered that the signature on the paperwork at the removal firm was a forgery.

Detectives learned that the man claiming to be Mr Baker had called into the shop and asked for £400 for the contents of the farmhouse. They agreed on £300 and the man was given £100 in lieu of payment. The detectives, along with Mr Libman, headed for a shop in nearby Uppermill, where the removal men had taken some of the furniture that 'Mr Baker' had asked to be dropped off. A local constable told the detectives the shop was rented by 24-year-old car salesman John Gartside.

As the men drove out of Uppermill they spotted Baker's car on a garage forecourt. A man was standing in front of the car, and Libman identified him as the man claiming to be Baker. Asked for his identity, the man said his name was Percy Baker. The local constable, however, knew his real identity.

'I know you,' he said. 'Your name is John Gartside.' Despite protestations to the contrary, Gartside was taken into custody pending further enquiries. He continued to try and bluff his way out of the situation by stating that Baker was indeed separating from his wife, that he had impersonated Mr Baker at Baker's request, 'to speed up the deal with Mr Libman', that he had bought the car off Baker on the previous Friday for £200, and bought the furniture for a similar amount a day or so later. He could show no receipts for these transactions, nor had he any evidence to back up his claims.

Detectives then searched both Manor House Farm and Gartside's house. The suspect lived with his parents less than 300 yards from Manor House Farm on the main Oldham to Huddersfield road, and from his bedroom window officers could clearly see the Baker's house.

In Gartside's bedroom detectives found a suit that showed faint traces of what appeared to be blood, along with a 0.38 Webley revolver taken from the bedside cabinet. At Manor House Farm, police found bloodstains on the walls, which were confirmed as human. Detectives then told Gartside that they believed he had murdered either Mr or Mrs Baker.

'What if it is both?' Gartside said coldly, before making a statement in which he claimed that he had called to see Baker about buying the car when he was offered the chance to buy some bedroom furniture. He claimed that Mrs Baker seemed to object to this but he sensed that they had been arguing before his arrival, and judging from a remark Baker made, his wife had been having an affair.

He then said that Baker had brought a loaded rifle and revolver downstairs, which he was going to show Gartside, and put them on the hall settee. Gartside said that Mrs Baker had then come into the room in a rage and had picked up a poker intent on striking her husband with it. He then claimed that Baker picked up the gun and shot his wife dead, whereupon Gartside tried to wrestle the gun from him and it went off, hitting the old man in the head.

Percy and Alice Baker. (TNA PRO)

'Spiv and wide-boy' John Gartside. (Author's collection)

'I then panicked. He was making a great deal of noise, writhing about in agony, so I picked up the rifle and shot him twice to put him out of his misery. There was blood all over the place!'

The next day, following a statement by Gartside, officers searched a place known as Brun Moor, half a mile from Manor House Farm, and discovered the naked bodies of Percy and Alice Baker in a shallow grave.

On Monday 28 July, John Gartside appeared before Mr Justice Pritchard at Leeds Assizes. The Crown had built up a strong case against Gartside, picking away at inconsistencies in his statement and discrediting his claim that Baker had been accidentally shot during a struggle. Forensic evidence found that from the trajectory of the bullet it was a physical impossibility for Baker to have shot himself in the head, as Gartside claimed.

The prosecution claimed that Gartside, dubbed a 'spiv and a wide-boy' in court, had kept an eye on the Baker's house, waiting for the opportunity to burgle the place. On the night of the murder he had gone to the house carrying his guns and during the course of a robbery he was disturbed. Mrs Baker came into the house first, saw Gartside and began to scream, and in order to silence her he shot her dead. He then had no choice but to execute Percy Baker when he rushed into the house. Instead of panicking at what he had done, the killer then coolly plotted the scheme of pretending the couple had separated and tried to pass himself off as Percy Baker. He was convicted on the third day of his trial and sentenced to death. There was no appeal and three weeks later Gartside went to the gallows.

74

SOME FORM OF INSANITY

George Henry Whelpton, 7 January 1948

It was shortly after midday, Friday 19 October 1947, when a neighbour noticed that the back door of the house belonging to Mrs Alison Parkin, on Wainwright Road, Doncaster, was wide open. She went to investigate and what she found when she stepped inside would haunt her for the rest of her life. On the kitchen floor lay the body of 15-year-old Maurice Parkin, his features grotesquely distorted, his tongue hanging from his bloated and battered face.

She hurried to call the police, and when officers searched the rest of the house they were met with a truly horrific scene. In the adjoining living room were the bodies of Maurice's mother and sister, 49-year-old Alison Parkin and 23-year-old Joyce Parkin. Cause of death was initially hard to estimate as all the victims had been stripped and subjected to brutal sexual mutilation. Their bodies had been sexually mutilated with a knife, and faeces, urine and blood were smeared across them and on the furniture and bedding. Two bloodstained knives were also recovered from the bedroom. A post-mortem found that all three had first been strangled.

Mrs Parkin's boyfriend, 31-year-old bus driver George Whelpton, was the prime suspect. With a fine physique and good looks, Whelpton was a popular man with many friends and had served with distinction with the Desert Rats, where, after emerging unscathed from a fierce attack, he earned the nickname 'Lucky George'. He was arrested at his place of work later that night.

'We are investigating the murders of Alison Parkin and two of her children at their home, and we believe you may be able to help us with our enquiries,' officers told him.

'Yes, that's right, I do. We had a row and I did it. I just can't remember all that happened.' Whelpton claimed he had had a quarrel with Mrs Parkin and he had hit her. Her son, awoken by the commotion, had come down and Whelpton had hit him also, and he had done the same when Joyce also came downstairs.

'I don't remember anything more. I left the house while it was dark and caught a trackless bus to Balby and went to my mother's house at Edlington.'

The truth of what had taken place that evening was revealed when Whelpton stood trial before Mr Justice Morris at Leeds in December. He was indicted only for the murder of Mrs Parkin, but evidence relating to the other murders would be called on by both prosecuting and defence counsel. Prosecution described the prisoner as 'a perfectly normal man in every respect' who had committed a murder as macabre and horrible it is hard to recall.

Whelpton's mother was called and told how her son had received serious head injuries in 1936 following a motorcycle accident. From then on he behaved 'queerly', often after a drink, and that his conduct at times terrified his family. Also speaking up for Whelpton was his wife, Irene. They had

Alison Parkin's house on Wainwright Road, Doncaster. (Author's Collection)

George Henry Whelpton. (Author's collection)

married during the war and had six children, although the long periods of separation put a strain on their relationship, and when Whelpton returned from the war they soon split up.

Whelpton began to spend more and more time on nightshifts, and spent other nights at his mother's. He had by this time begun an affair with Alison Parkin. His wife also supported his mother's admissions that her husband was suffering from some form of insanity, and said that on a number of occasions he had passed out after drinking.

The court then heard of events leading up to the murders. On the night of 9 October 1947, Whelpton had gone for a drink with Alison, along with her sister and husband. Although nearly twenty years older than him, Alison and Whelpton enjoyed a good relationship and he got on well with her children and friends. They were last seen shortly after closing time walking arm-in-arm together down Wainwright Road.

Joyce arrived home at around 11.25 p.m. and stood kissing her boyfriend at the front door until her mother called from inside and they then parted. At a few minutes past six the following morning, a workmate of Joyce's made her usual call to the house, but, unable to raise anyone, she tried the door, found it locked and went on alone to work.

Whelpton gave various accounts of what had happened in the house. In one he claimed that he had been upstairs in bed with Joyce when Alison had caught them, and in another he said that after the children had gone to bed he had supper with Alison and they had then gone into the sitting room where she asked him for some money. She told him that her previous 'bloke' gave her money and this started a quarrel.

> She picked something up and tried to strike me with it. I caught hold of her and she dropped to the floor. I could not make her talk to me. I was frightened and ran outside and I met her son in the kitchen… I hit him… he fell on the floor and would not talk to me either. I then saw the daughter in the living room… I then hit her and I don't remember anything else.

Summing up, Mr Justice Morris said the main issue was whether Whelpton was insane as his counsel claimed, or was he, as the Crown alleged, a brutal killer who had committed horrific crimes for sexual gratification.

'Just because there may be an absence of motive, as the defence had claimed, that itself does not prove insanity,' he told the jury, who needed just twenty minutes to find Whelpton guilty as charged. 'Thank you,' he smiled, as his fate was sealed.

There was no appeal and Whelpton was hanged by fellow Doncaster man Steve Wade, a man he knew well. Wade noted that his erstwhile friend had met his end bravely.

75

HANGED ON HIS BIRTHDAY

Arthur George Osborne, 30 December 1948

Despite his advancing years, 70-year-old Ernest Hargreaves Westwood still led an active life. Widowed shortly after the end of the war, Ernie, as he liked to be known, now lived alone at 'Craggan', a small end terraced house on Law Lane, Southowram, Halifax, but instead of enjoying retirement he had chosen to busy himself in a number of jobs. Besides working full-time as a foreman mason at a Halifax carpet manufacturer, he also supplemented his income acting as a debt collector in the evenings for a local doctor.

On Friday evening, 24 September 1948, neighbour Emily Hainsworth called round for a chat and noticed that the old man seemed quite frail. She advised him to rest but Ernie told her had to go out again that night collecting, and as she bade him good evening she arranged to pop around tomorrow to help with some chores.

'Craggan', Law Lane, Southowram. (TNA PRO)

The following morning, Emily noticed the curtains at his house were still drawn at 11 a.m., and when she tried the door she found it unlocked. Entering the hall she called out and, finding no answer, made her way upstairs, where she found Ernie lying in his bed in a pool of blood and suffering from terrible head injuries. As the old man was rushed to hospital, and when the old man died from his injuries detectives launched a murder investigation. They quickly surmised that the attacker had probably gained entry by breaking the window at the side of the house. It was here they got their first clue, when a clear set of fingerprints was found on the window ledge. Copies were made and sent away to see if a match could be found. With drawers emptied out onto the floor, it seemed that robbery was the motive.

That same morning, at a house a few streets away, a letter arrived at the home of Edna Green. 'I have been to your place but I see you was not up. I will be back on Monday or Tuesday.' It was signed Arthur Osborne, a young man who had called a number of times over the past couple of days and who on the previous day had made references to the old man; how he lived alone and that he must have a lot of money. When she heard of the murder Edna wasted no time in contacting the police.

Osborne was 27 years old, married with three young children, but with his wife now in a mental hospital and the children in care. In fact, as detectives launched the murder enquiry, Osborne was travelling down to Chichester, West Sussex, where he and his new fiancée had arranged to be married. Arrangements had been made: the church booked and honeymoon organised when Osborne sent a telegram warning he may be delayed. Hearing this, his fiancée then cancelled all plans for that day and when Osborne finally arrived in Sussex he was shown the reports of the murder, which named him as the man police wished to interview.

Explaining that it must be a mistake, Osborne said he would return to Yorkshire to clear his name, and the following morning caught a train north. The police were notified of Osborne's plans and he was soon under arrest.

The killer gained entry by forcing the side window. (TNA PRO)

Police photograph of Arthur George Osborne. (T.J. Leech Archive)

H.M. Prison,
Leeds.
21st Dec., 1948.

2078 Arthur George Osborne.

Dear Sir,

I have today received telephoned instructions that the Home Secretary is not to interfere with the sentence of death passed on the above-named. Pending the receipt of the official confirmation, the Under Sheriff has fixed the date of execution provisionally as Thursday, 30th Instant.

I will forward the usual forms and railway warrant and confirm the date within the next day or so. In the meantime, will you please confirm that you can attend. I enclose a stamped addressed envelope.

Yours faithfully,

Governor.

Mr Allen,
 Rawson Arms Hotel,
  Peel Street,
   Farnworth,
    Bolton, Lancs.

The letter informing the executioners of the details relating to Osborne's execution. (Author's collection)

Osborne's telltale fingerprints. (TNA PRO)

Assistant hangman Harry Allen recorded the details of Osborne's execution. (Author's collection)

Osborne's prints matched those found at the scene of the murder, and he made a statement admitting that he had gone to the house intending to steal from Westwood. He had forced open the window with a screwdriver, and quickly located some money in a box. Not satisfied, he crept upstairs when he heard a voice and something was thrown at him. Fearing for his safety, Osborne claimed he lashed out in a panic and must have killed Westwood accidentally.

He was convicted before Mr Justice Slade on 30 November and hanged one month later. It was Osborne's 28th birthday.

76

THE BOYFRIEND

Dennis Neville, 2 June 1949

'They've found the body of a young girl on the cricket field behind Calderbank Mill… the place is swarming with police,' the man breathed excitedly as he rushed into the bar at Dewsbury Moor Working Men's Club.

It was Sunday morning, 20 February 1949, when a milkman walking his dog had discovered the body lying near a wall. The victim was partially dressed; her face bloodstained, and there were scratches on her neck and right breast. A doctor recorded that cause of death was strangulation and that she had been dead for approximately twelve hours.

She was soon identified as 21-year-old Marian Poskett, and inquires into her last movements led officers to Dennis Neville, Marian's sometime-boyfriend, who had been seen walking with her towards the cricket field on the previous night. After initially denying any involvement in the murder, Neville suddenly blurted out, 'Forget what I said before. I did it. I will tell you the truth now.'

Marian Poskett's body was found in a field at Dewsbury. (TNA PRO)

He then confessed that that they had walked through Dewsbury, along Watergate, onto the cricket field:

We talked for a while and then I took hold of her neck in my right hand and sunk my fingers into her throat. She lay back without making any sound. She was still breathing. I thumped her on the jaw and also in the throat with the side of my hand.

Neville stood trial at Leeds Assizes on Monday 9 May, and despite his confession, his defence counsel focused on his tragic background to try to justify his actions and appeal to the sympathy of the jury.

His counsel told the court that at the age of just 14, Neville had left school and enlisted in the army until his true age was discovered and he was discharged. In July 1943, as soon as he was legally old enough to serve, he enlisted again and took part in the Normandy landings in 1944, and during this time he was diagnosed as schizophrenic, but before he could be treated

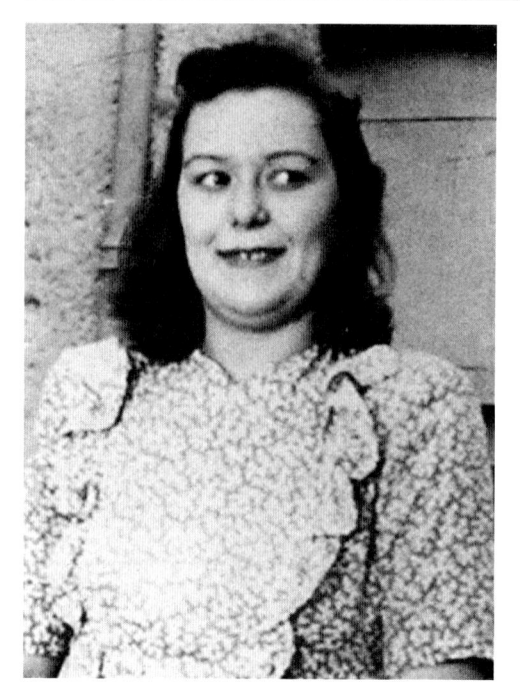

Marian Poskett. (TNA PRO)

he was taken as a prisoner of war. As a result of his mental illness, Neville spent a great deal of time in solitary confinement and received heavy beatings.

Following his release, he returned to Dewsbury, where he discovered his brother had been killed in action and his parents had separated. A few days later his father was killed in a street fight by a local tough, who had then threatened Neville with the same if he said anything to the police.

Examined by various doctors, Neville had been found to be an emotional wreck, and diagnosed as frightened and impulsive, with a resentful and intolerable attitude. He was recommended for admittance to a local mental hospital, but after explaining his home circumstances, and how he would be leaving his mother and two young sisters alone; it was arranged for him to become an outpatient at Leeds General Hospital.

As for a motive, the court heard that Neville and Marian had been friends since primary school and had been courting since he left the army. It seemed clear that Marian was keener on Neville than he appeared to be on her, and when, in the autumn of 1948, she had made it clear that she wanted to marry him, he broke off their relationship.

When she told later told him she was pregnant by a chap called 'Ronnie', rather than avoid any contact with her, Neville seemed to re-kindle the relationship and again began sexual relations with Marian. Marian then told him that she would name him as the father and that he would have to marry her. The prosecution stated that this was the crux of the case. They had then gone to the cricket field where, after having sex, they had had a quarrel, which ended when Neville punched Marian in the face before strangling her.

The defence had pleaded that a reasonable man may well have lost control in these circumstances, but following Mr Justice Finnemore's guidance the jury needed just one hour to return a guilty verdict. There were gasps of shock and surprise in the public gallery as the verdict was returned. Neville neglected to appeal, instead relying on a petition for mercy, which received over 7,000 signatures. It was to no avail.

MURDER CHARGE AGAINST WESTTOWN MAN

DEWSBURY MOOR WOMAN WAS STRANGLED

—INQUEST EVIDENCE

The discovery on Sunday morning of the body of Marian Poskitt (21), of Low Road, Dewsbury Moor, lying in St. Matthew's cricket field in Watergate, behind the Calder Bank Mill of Messrs. E. Fox and Sons, was followed by rapid developments, for late on Sunday evening Supt. Arthur Iveson, of Dewsbury Borough Police Force, announced that a man had been arrested and charged with the murder of Miss Poskitt.

On Monday morning at a special sitting of Dewsbury Magistrates' Court, Dennis Neville (22), glazier's labourer, of 40, Manor Road, Westtown, made a brief appearance in the dock, during which he was charged with the murder of Miss Poskitt. He was Mrs. Poskitt, he decided to visit the police station, where his worst fears were justified.

Miss Poskitt was the second of four daughters. Educated at St. John's School, Dewsbury Moor, and later at Teinplefield School, she had been in the Land Army for a time, but because of a leg injury she came out and recently had been employed as a weaver, by Messrs Wormalds and Walker Ltd., Britannia Mills.

She is said to have been lively and very fond of dancing and the news of her tragic death was received as a shock by her workmates.

It is known that Neville and Miss Poskitt had been on friendly terms for some months.

Newscutting relating to the murder of Marian Poskett. (T.J. Leech Archive)

77

GANGSTERS

Walter Sharpe, 30 March 1950

It was shortly after 10 a.m. on the morning of 16 November 1949, when 52-year-old Abraham Harry Levine, known locally as 'Old Abe', opened the Albion Watch Depot, his small lock-up jeweller's shop on Albion Street, Leeds. He had barely raised the shutters when two young men entered and placed a number of cheap service-issue watches on the counter.

'Do you want to buy these?' one asked, and when Levine said he did not, both men pulled out revolvers and told him to 'hand over the money.'

Although the till contained just a few pounds, Levine was not prepared to meekly hand over his money, and, ordering them to leave his shop, he came from behind the counter and attempted to grab at the younger of the two. As the two men grappled, the other brought the butt of his gun down on the shopkeeper's head. As his friend broke free from Levine's grip, the other of the two fired twice, leaving the old man slumped against the counter as they fled into the street.

Taken to Leeds Infirmary, Levine told police, 'one man hit me on the head, the other shot me,' before drifting into a coma. Although he was able to make a statement describing his attackers, he soon lapsed into unconsciousness and died the following day.

Two days after the shooting, detectives in Southport spoke to two youths who had been picked up for loitering. Asked for identification, they gave their names as 19-year-old Walter Sharpe

Albion Watch Depot, where Abe Levine was shot dead. (TNA PRO)

and 17-year-old Gordon Lannen, both with addresses in Leeds. Taken into custody on suspicion of being involved in the murder, they were questioned separately and Lannen immediately confessed.

'We did the Leeds job… but I didn't shoot him. He was shouting and we both hit him to keep him quiet. Then my pal shot him.'

Lannen said that they had burned their raincoats and thrown two revolvers and bullets into a river near Southport. Faced with this confession and the fact that Sharpe had a number of bullets in his jacket pocket, both were charged with the murder and returned to Leeds to face trial.

Described in the local press as 'gangsters', they stood trial before Mr Justice Streatfeild on 9 March 1950. The trial had a sensational start when Lannen announced that he wished to plead guilty. His counsel told the judge that the plea was entirely contrary to what he had been advised and a plea of not guilty was then entered.

The case for the prosecution was that the two accused had set out in common adventure to rob Mr Levine. Each had a loaded gun, either to frighten the victim into submission or to render him incapable of resistance, or to resist arrest. One or both had then struck him over the head with the butt of a revolver and one had shot him in the stomach, and that Lannen had freely confessed to the murder.

In his defence, Sharpe made an attempt to state that the shooting was an accident. He said that when Levine had grabbed hold of his panicking friend, Sharpe had tried to intervene, and during the struggle the gun had gone off accidentally. He claimed that he didn't know that the gun had gone off at first. Defence counsel attempted to show that Sharpe had been influenced in his actions by watching violent movies at the cinema. He was said to visit the cinema three times a week and had fallen under the influence of 'those terrible gangster films'.

On the second day of the trial the jury needed less than twenty minutes to find both men guilty. Sentence was passed first on Lannen, who, due to his age, came under the protection of the Children and Young Persons Act.

'Because you are under the age of eighteen you cannot suffer the supreme penalty of the law. That act protects even young gangsters. You shall be detained until the King's pleasure be known,' the judge told him.

As Lannen was removed from the dock, a black cap was draped upon the judge's wig and he passed sentence on Sharpe: 'For your part in this most shocking crime it is my duty to pass upon you, young as you are, the sentence which is prescribed by law for this offence.'

Walter Sharpe was the last person to be hanged in the old execution shed on A Wing.

Sharpe's fascination with the violent Hollywood movies, 'those wretched gangster films' as the judge had labelled them, had been blamed for him committing the murder. Later that year, Ealing Films produced the classic melodramatic police film *The Blue Lamp*, which featured two young villains robbing a jeweller's shop. Sharp-eyed viewers may notice in the montage of actual newspaper headlines shown in the film's introduction, actual headlines pertaining to the murder of Abraham Levine.

78

TO CATCH A THIEF

Alfred Moore, 6 February 1952

Detectives in the West Riding Police Force suspected that Alfred Moore had a secret pastime. Although he earned a reasonable income as a poultry-farmer from his secluded home at Whinney Close Farm, Kirkheaton, a few miles from Huddersfield, he seemed to be living well above his means as a farmer. For one, his children travelled daily by taxi to an expensive private school, and the farmhouse was stocked with furniture and artefacts seemingly well beyond the means of a normal Yorkshire farmer. They also suspected that he was responsible for over a hundred unsolved burglaries in the area.

Alfred Moore. (Author's collection)

PC Alfred Jagger. (Author's collection)

It was due to past misdemeanours that Moore had first come to the attention of detectives faced with a growing list of unsolved crimes that summer of 1951. During the war, Moore had decided that he had no wish to fight for king and country and absconded from his unit. In May 1947, he was arrested on suspicion of a robbery committed nearly four years earlier, but when the case came to trial he was acquitted. The resultant press coverage, however, had come to the attention of the Military Police, and when Moore was formally discharged at Leeds Assizes, he was immediately re-arrested and charged with desertion. Taken into custody, it was a matter of routine that his photograph was taken and put on file, and it was this 'mug shot' that played a pivotal role in events that took place four years later.

At 45 years old, Detective Inspector Duncan 'Sandy' Fraser, the head of Huddersfield CID, had over twenty-two years service, but for the last couple of years he had become increasingly frustrated by the growing number of unsolved burglaries and break-ins at local mills and offices. Fraser's main suspect was Alfred Moore, and he arranged for him to be kept under observation. On the night of Saturday 14 July 1951, suspecting that Moore was out 'on the job', a ten-man team set a trap to catch a thief. Officers threw a cordon around Whinney Close Farm, which they hoped would, on his return, catch the thief red-handed.

The police, shown the 'mug shot' photograph of Moore to aid recognition, were posted in pairs, each equipped with binoculars, a torch and police whistle. From 11.45 p.m. that night, all roads to the farm were sealed off with no one able to come or go without being spotted.

Simple as it was, the plan failed. At shortly before 2 a.m., five shots rang out across the field and Inspector Fraser and Constable Alf Jagger lay mortally wounded, 80 yards apart and less than 350 yards from the house. Inspector Fraser died from his injuries at the scene, while PC Jagger lay bleeding heavily from gunshot wounds to the stomach. He was able to tell a colleague that Moore had shot him before collapsing into unconsciousness. Hordes of police then converged on the farmhouse and smoke was seen to billow from a chimney.

'Come out, we are police officers,' they demanded, knocking loudly at the door. Moore's wife answered and asked what they wanted. Told they wanted to speak to her husband, Moore then answered the door dressed in a pair of flannel pyjamas and a pair of Wellington boots.

Placed under arrest, he was charged with shooting two police officers. Moore protested his innocence and, when asked if he had a gun, he produced a shotgun, the only weapon he owned, which was taken away for forensic examination. It was not the murder weapon.

Moore was then placed under arrest and taken into custody. A search of the fields and farmhouse failed to locate the murder weapon and, with nothing to directly prove that Moore had carried out the shootings, an identity parade was arranged for the benefit of the dying constable. Eight men of similar height and build to Moore were gathered together and paraded before Jagger. The constable immediately pointed to Moore, who was then charged with the murder of Inspector Fraser. It became a double murder when PC Jagger died from his injuries during the night.

Alfred Moore stood trial before Mr Justice Pearson shortly before Christmas 1951. Following his arrest, detectives had combed the farmhouse looking for the murder weapon and other evidence linking him with the murders, but without success. They did find a tremendous amount of stolen property linking him with many of the unsolved burglaries that Inspector Fraser had been investigating.

The case hinged on the deathbed identification made by PC Jagger, although there was nothing else to connect the prisoner, and the prosecution told the court that Jagger had been shown a photograph of Moore shortly before the identification parade.

The jury needed less than an hour to return a guilty verdict and Moore was sentenced to death.

'I am not guilty,' he cried out after the verdict was delivered, and continued to protest his innocence to the last. On the eve of his execution, he spent the night maintaining his innocence loudly in between crying out his wife's name. Interest in his execution was overshadowed in that day's newspapers following the death of King George VI, who had passed away a few hours before Moore walked to the gallows.

Was Alfred Moore a callous double murderer, or the victim of wrongful identification? Maybe the killer had been a 'friend' of Moore's, perhaps a fence calling at the house to do some 'business' and he had stumbled into the police cordon. He may then have shot the officers and fled from the murder scene the way he had come as the officers closed ranks and circled the farmhouse. Locals who remembered the shootings claimed that Moore was innocent and that they knew the real identity of the killer.

In 2008, a retired police officer researching the case even went so far as to name the real killer as Clifford Mead, a former 'friend' of Alfred Moore. Mead was alleged to have boasted to friends many years after the event that he had killed the officers and he still had the murder weapon. Perhaps a review of the evidence will clear the name of Alfred Moore? Thief? Maybe. But murderer?

79

IN THE NICK OF TIME

Philip Henry, 30 July 1953

As George Laughton left to go to work on the morning of 10 March 1953, he noticed that someone had removed a wooden shutter that covered the scullery window at his home at 32 Diamond Street, York. As he made his way up the path towards the back gate, he turned and looked back and noticed that the bedroom window of the house next door, No. 30, was wide open. Later that afternoon, his wife came home from work and, looking over the fence, discovered the naked body of their neighbour, 76-year-old Flora Jane Gilligan.

When detectives arrived at the house, it initially appeared as though the elderly lady had tragically fallen from the upstairs window, but it soon became clear that this was a case of foul play. A post-mortem revealed that Flora had been raped and an attempt had been made to strangle her, before the killer had thrown her from the bedroom window, causing fatal head injuries. It appeared that he had entered the house via the kitchen, presumably after failing to gain entry next door. A large footprint was left on a laundry basket beneath the kitchen window, but more interesting was the fingerprints left on the window frame. With the aid of Wakefield Fingerprint Bureau, copies were made and detectives began to make enquires to find a match.

One of the first groups of people to be fingerprinted were soldiers stationed at nearby Strensall Army Camp. The training camp had a transient population with units coming and going on a weekly basis, as men were trained in various skills before being posted overseas. Detectives struck lucky at once when an identical match was discovered belonging to Philip Henry, a 25-year-old West Indian-born soldier in the King's Own Yorkshire Light Infantry.

Henry strenuously denied any involvement. He claimed not to know the location of Diamond Street, and said that on the night of the murder he had caught the last bus to camp from the railway station. Enquiries could not produce any travellers on that bus to support Henry's alibi, nor his comrades, who failed to confirm he had been in his quarters by midnight, as Henry claimed.

A check on his uniform revealed wooden splinters identical to ones on the bedroom window frame, and Henry's boots also matched the print left at the house.

Although it was all circumstantial evidence, it was nonetheless comprehensive and three months later Henry found himself before Mr Justice Jones at York Assizes. The trial had a sensational climax when the jury asked the judge if they could visit the scene of the crime before reaching a verdict.

The body of Flora Gilligan outside her home in Diamond Street, York. (TNA PRO)

Killer Philip Henry was arrested just days before he was due to be posted overseas. (T.J. Leech Archive)

Mr Justice Jones claimed never to have heard such a request before, but he agreed to lay on a coach to ferry them to Diamond Street. They spent just thirty minutes at the house before returning to the court, and, after a further deliberation, they found the prisoner guilty as charged.

Henry had been arrested in the nick of time. His unit was due to be posted overseas a few days after his arrest. They left without him, and at the end of July he was hanged. His execution was unusual, as it marked the only occasion in which the infamous hangman Albert Pierrepoint officiated at Leeds Prison.

80

PAYBACK

Robert William Moore, 5 January 1954

Twenty-seven-year-old Robert Moore was thought by all his acquaintances as a charming, easygoing, likeable man. Born in Canada, he had moved to England with his mother when he was just five years old, and did a variety of jobs before being called up to the army, only to be quickly discharged on medical grounds, as he suffered from asthma. Moore became a taxi driver and eventually saved up enough money to buy his own vehicle and he soon drifted into dealing in second-hand cars.

On 23 April 1953, Moore purchased a car from fellow second-hand dealer, Edward Watson, whom he was knew from the various car auctions both men frequented. Moore paid the asking price of £55 and took the car away, only to discover the car was defective and not worth the money he had paid for it. Being sold as seen, he negotiated with Watson to sell the car back to him, but it was at a loss and Moore harboured a grudge against Watson as a result.

On Saturday 30 May, Watson was seen at a Leeds car auction with a large amount of cash on him. Moore, also at the auction, offered to take Watson to Harrogate to look at a car that he had heard was for sale. The two arranged to meet the next day at 10.30 a.m. Watson left home the following morning to keep the appointment, but was never seen alive again. His wife reported him missing to the police on 2 June. She also contacted Moore to see if he knew where her husband could be. Moore said that Watson had failed to keep his appointment that Sunday morning.

Police investigating Watson's disappearance visited Moore's home and spotted a shovel and a gun in the back of his car, which was parked on the drive. When they asked Watson about the items, Moore laughingly said, 'You don't think I have shot and buried him do you?'

No sooner had the police left, than Moore attempted suicide, by putting his head in a gas

Robert Moore. (Author's Collection)

Ted Watson. (Author's collection)

The car in which Robert Moore lured Ted Watson to his death. (TNA PRO)

oven. It proved unsuccessful and he was taken to Harrogate hospital, but on his discharged later that same day he was arrested by the police. Moore then confessed that he had indeed shot and buried Watson, and had then repaid a large loan to his aunt.

He then took police to a lonely spot in Fewston and pointed to a shallow grave. They found the body of Ted Watson: he had been shot five times at point blank range.

During his trial before Mr Justice Stable, Moore claimed that he had shot Watson accidentally while trying to shoot a pheasant that he had spotted near his car. He said that he had found the money on Watson's body by chance and that he had taken it just in case he needed to flee the country.

Although suspected of being involved in the disappearance, if Watson hadn't attempted suicide it seems unlikely that the police would have ever discovered Watson's body as it was so well hidden in a remote location.

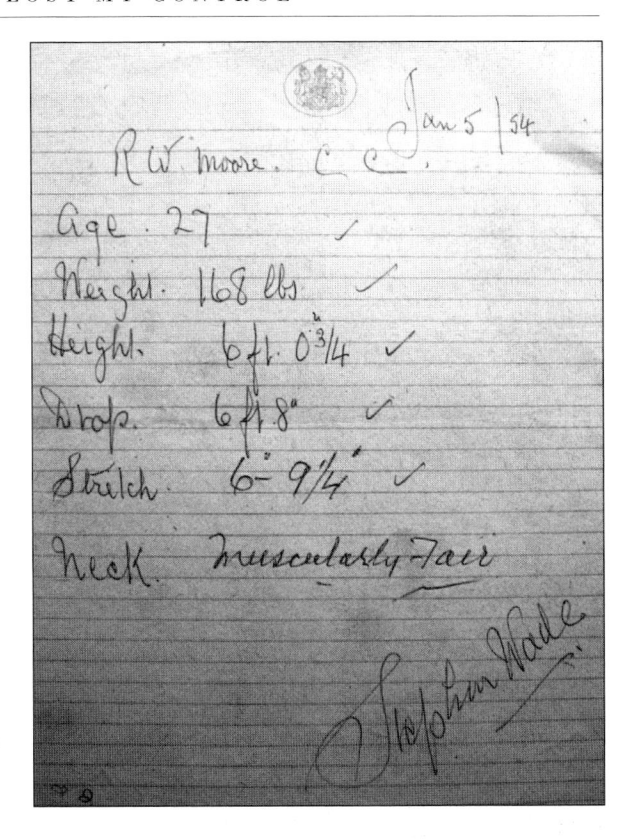

Steve Wade's handwritten details regarding the execution of Robert Moore. (Author's collection)

81

'I LOST MY CONTROL'

Wilhelm Lubina, 27 January 1954

Charlotte Ball and her husband ran a lodging house on Springfield Street in Barnsley, where Wilhelm Lubina, a 42-old-year-old Polish miner, had lived for a number of years. Over time Lubina had struck up a close friendship with Mrs Ball, who was of German origin, and Lubina, who spoke fluent German, was able to converse with her in her native tongue. For Lubina though, the relationship was far more than just friendship and he grew to love Charlotte.

On 25 June 1953, Charlotte's husband was returning home along with an acquaintance, when, as they approached the house, they heard Charlotte screaming. Both men rushed inside where they found her moaning and staggering about in the kitchen, covered in blood. Also in the room was Lubina, who was clutching a knife in his hand. As soon as Lubina saw Charlotte's husband, he rushed into another room and started repeatedly stabbing himself in the chest and head with the knife.

When the police arrived, Mrs Ball was found to have died from her wounds, but Lubina was taken to hospital and treated for injuries which were not life threatening. When he had recovered he was

The Ball's lodging house on Springfield Street, Barnsley. (Author's collection)

Charlotte Ball. (Author's collection)

taken to Barnsley police station, where he was charged with murder. Lubina confessed that he had killed Charlotte and that he wanted no defence. He said that on an earlier occasion he and Mrs Ball had had a fierce quarrel and that she had started hitting him and kicking him.

He said, 'I told her that I never hit a woman before and did not want a woman to hit me.' He said Charlotte had then promised never to do it again. He said that on the day of the murder they had quarrelled again and he said simply, 'I lost my control.'

Before Mr Justice Stable at the Leeds Assizes, Lubina never denied the murder but said that he had not planned to do it. The prosecution said that witnesses had seen him sharpening the murder weapon whilst at work, and this implied that the murder was premeditated.

82

SUSPECT NUMBER ONE

Albert George Hall, 22 April 1954

The investigation had slowly ground to another dead end. After sixteen days of fruitless searching, during which time police officers had dragged reservoirs, lifted tombstones and combed derelict buildings, detectives in Halifax decided to call in the assistance of Scotland Yard. They were investigating the disappearance of 12-year-old Mary Hackett, who had vanished whilst playing outside her home at 6 Cemetery Lodge, Lister Lane, Halifax.

The following day, Saturday 29 August 1954, Detective Superintendent John Ball, and his assistant, Detective Sergeant Dennis Hawkins, travelled north to take over the investigation. Mary had been missing since Wednesday lunchtime, 12 August, and as the two Scotland Yard men sifted through the evidence already collated they decided to speak to the caretaker of the Park Congregational Church, which stood almost directly opposite Mary's home on Lister Lane.

Albert George Hall had only begun his job as caretaker at the Park Congregational Church on Monday 10 August, two days before Mary vanished from her home. The crypt of the church contained a vast catacomb of cellars and had been used as an air-raid shelter during the war, when over 1,000 locals had taken shelter following threats of enemy raids. It had already been searched twice by police officers since Mary's disappearance. The new caretaker had greeted the police with a smile and had been most co-operative with the investigators, even providing tea and biscuits as they searched the dark and dusty vaults.

Ball and Hawkins organised a third search of the crypt and met for the first time the 47-year-old caretaker. Once again Hall offered the detectives tea and biscuits and as the search was taking place Superintendent Ball noticed that in one corner of the crypt stood two new tins of paint, opened. He asked about them, and Hall told him they had been bought to repaint the vestry. Hall was advised to replace the lids before the paint dried up, and with his ever-present smile he told the detective he had misplaced the lids and they had probably been thrown away with the rubbish. During a conversation with the detectives, Hall had also mentioned that he remembered hearing voices in the church on the day Mary disappeared.

This immediately rang alarm bells with the experienced Scotland Yard men, and from that moment Hall became suspect number one. Why had he not mentioned the voices earlier? Also, as a caretaker, Hall should be used to the general upkeep of the church and its outbuildings, and it seemed highly unlikely any handyman would lose one lid from a new tin of paint, let alone two. Superintendent Ball pondered this with his sergeant and they concluded that the paint must have been placed to mask some other, perhaps more sinister smell.

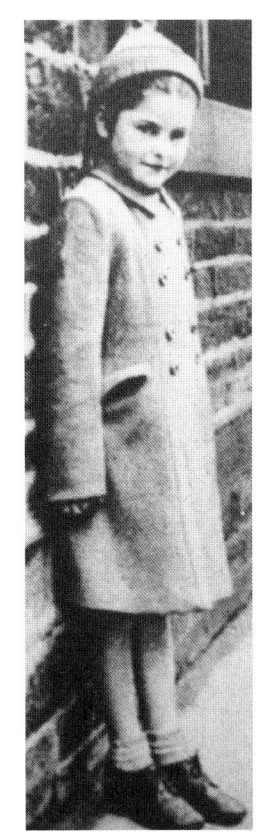

Mary Hackett. (Author's Collection)

139

Newscutting relating to the Halifax murder. (T.J. Leech Archive)

Caretaker Albert George Hall was always the main suspect. (Author's collection)

On 21 September they returned for another search of the church crypt. Armed this time with a team of several officers carrying heavy digging tools and arc lights, the smile now vanished from Hall's face when he saw the size of the search party. He made a futile attempt to stop them gaining access and stood by helplessly as the new search began. Soon the mystery of the disappearance of Mary Hackett was solved. Mary was discovered in a shallow grave in the crypt: she had been battered about the head and her skull fractured by repeated heavy blows.

There was as yet no hard evidence against Hall, so a round-the-clock surveillance was put on him. The following day, Hall was followed to Scalebor Park Hospital, a mental asylum at nearby Burley-in-Wharfdale. As he left, detectives interviewed Dr James Valentine, who told them Hall was a former patient and had come to see him to ask his advice as he was suspected of being involved in the young girl's death.

Hall had told the doctor details of Mary's injuries that only the killer and a number of high-ranking officers knew, and, satisfied he was their man, Hall was finally arrested and charged with murder. 'Very well, I have been expecting it,' he told the arresting officers.

At his four-day trial before Mr Justice Pearson at Leeds Assizes in March, Hall was described as a 'glib liar' who had attempted to befriend the detectives involved in the case. They had waited patiently for the evidence to connect him with the murder and that had come when he had spoken to Dr Valentine shortly after the body was discovered. Only the killer could have had known the details of the injuries on the dead girl, and after hearing all the evidence, it took the jury just over six hours before finding Hall guilty.

83

THE LODGERS

Edward Lindsay Reid, 1 September 1954

Twenty-four-year-old Edward Reid and Arthur White, aged 60, were roommates at a hostel on Great Horton Road, Bradford. It was a busy lodging house with twenty-one male borders along with their landlady, Mrs Fairweather, her daughter and son-in-law, and their nephew.

Fellow tenants had already noticed that Reid and White had been quarrelling recently and on 3 April 1954, while sitting down to dinner, they had another heated argument, with Reid, in particular, appearing to be in a very bed temper. Later that evening they both went out drinking in the local pubs. Reid was seen returning to the boarding house at approximately 10.40 p.m.

Later that same evening, a fellow lodger returning to the house through the back yard came across a man, apparently unconscious, lying in a pool of blood. On closer inspection he recognised the man as Arthur White. When police arrived they found that White was dead, and it seemed he had fallen from an upper storey window.

They went to his room where they found Reid in a drunken state. There were bloodstains on the windowsill and on the guttering outside the window and Reid had blood on his face and on his sleeves, and a swollen right hand. Reid said that he had cut himself shaving, but he could not satisfactorily explain how his hands were so bloodied and swollen, and he was placed under arrest.

A post-mortem found that White had severe bruising, along with two broken legs, and his skull was fractured in two places. These injuries could have been consistent with an accidental fall from the window, but the pathologist also stated that some of his injuries were more than likely caused before the fall.

When Reid stood trial before Mr Justice Donovan at the Yorkshire Assizes at Leeds Town Hall that

The lodging house in Bradford, where Arthur White was murdered. (TNA PRO)

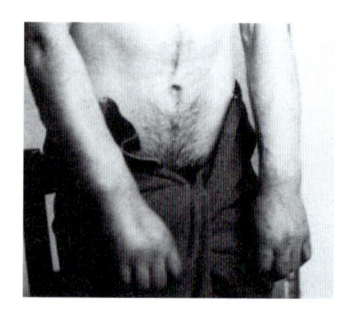

Police noticed that Reid's hands were badly swollen. This photograph was taken soon after he was taken into custody. (TNA PRO)

summer, he pleaded not guilty to White's murder. His defence claimed that Reid had no reason to murder White, and that no other lodger had heard any disturbance on the night White's body had been found. Reid had also stated that his bruised right hand had been caused by an accident at work. The prosecution, however, called his landlady to give evidence and she stated that when Reid had returned to his lodgings that night, she had not seen any blood on him. Despite continually protesting his innocence, Reid was found guilty of murder and sentenced to death.

84

THE SAFE HOUSE

Winston Shaw, 4 May 1955

Jean Cave Tate was a frightened woman. The 24-year-old had met 39-year-old Winston Shaw in the spring of 1951 and they soon began to live together as man and wife. Shaw had married before the war but was separated from, although still friends with, his wife. In the summer of 1954 things began to turn sour. Now a mother of two young children, relations between Jean and Shaw, an unemployed radio engineer of Shipley, West Riding, became so bad that she sought help from Social Services and, along with the children, she was offered sanctuary in a temporary 'safe house'.

That September Shaw persuaded her to return to him and they took lodgings together in Bradford. The reconciliation soon became a nightmare. Shaw had arranged for his first wife to take care of Jean's two children so that he and Jean could try to patch up their differences. In reality he became a brutal bully, keeping Jean a prisoner in the flat for several weeks until officers from the NSPCC discovered the truth and Jean was removed, reunited with her children, and taken to another safe house, this time a flat in a residential block at Knaresborough Hospital.

On Friday 3 December Shaw discovered her whereabouts and tried to persuade her to return to live with him. He called at the flat, taking presents for Jean and teddy bears for the children. The police were actually on site when Shaw arrived, and after telling him she did not want his gifts, nor to ever see him again, officers escorted Shaw from the flat. Shaw immediately took lodgings close to the hospital and later that evening he returned to the flat carrying an axe. Jean was found murdered later than night.

At 11.30 p.m. detectives called at his lodgings and took Shaw into custody under suspicion of the murder of Jean Tate. Shaw admitted that he had gone back to the flat in the hope of reconciliation, but on arrival he heard a man's voice from inside. As he entered, Shaw said the man picked up a chair and attacked him, at which Shaw fended him off with the axe he had brought along. During the struggle, Jean Tate had been fatally wounded. He could offer no real explanation as to why she had received six blows from an axe and had been stabbed twenty-five times.

At his three-day trial before Mr Justice Pearce in March 1955, Shaw maintained the story of accidentally striking Jean Tate whilst fending off an attacker. The prosecution tore his defence to pieces; why, if this was the case, had he not tried to call for assistance when he realised Jean had been injured, and if he had merely used the axe as he claimed, why was a bloodstained knife found in the bathroom at his lodgings?

85

THE MOTHER-IN-LAW

Alec Wilkinson, 12 August 1955

Alec Wilkinson, a Barnsley coal miner, and Maureen Farrell were both barely out of their teens when they married in the summer of 1954 and moved into their own home on Bradbury Back Walk, Wombwell. The house was on a row better known locally as Mitchell's Terrace, and living just a few doors away on the same street was Maureen's mother, Clara Farrell, a 50-year-old former prostitute, whom neighbours referred to as 'The Green Linnet'.

Although Mrs Farrell had initially been friendly and helpful towards the newlyweds as they set up their home, she soon turned on her son-in-law and began to make trouble between him and his wife. She consistently interfered in the relationship, accusing Wilkinson of being lazy, and tried several time to persuade Maureen to leave him.

In the spring of 1955, Maureen moved out and returned to her mother's. Whenever Wilkinson called to try to persuade Maureen to return to him, Mrs Farrell taunted her son-in-law, claiming that Maureen would rather become a prostitute that return to him.

On Saturday 30 April, Wilkinson spent the day drinking and, as the pubs closed, he moved on to a café where, over a cup of coffee, he considered his situation and decided to make one last chance at reconciliation. He was very drunk when he asked a taxi-driver to take him back to Mitchell's Terrace in the early hours of the following morning. As he approached his mother-in-law's house he could see Mrs Farrell through the thin curtains, standing in the front room and assumed she was waiting up for her daughter to arrive home. Sure enough, a few minutes later Maureen was one of a group of women who made their way down the street. Bidding her friends goodnight she entered the house, and seconds later Wilkinson approached the front door.

Mrs Farrell answered the door, and seeing Wilkinson she immediately launched into a stream of abuse. Wilkinson stood motionless on the doorstep until, finally, he snapped. He lashed out with his fist and knocked Clara Farrell to the floor. He then knelt over her prostrate body and began bashing her head repeatedly into the hard floor. His wife tried to pull him off her stricken mother, and Wilkinson responded by lashing out at Maureen, knocking her unconscious. He then went to the kitchen, returned with a carving knife, and began a horrific attack on his mother-in-law. As blood seeped across the thin carpet he piled cushions and furniture over her body and set it alight.

Alec Wilkinson and his wife Maureen at their wedding. He would later be convicted of killing his mother-in-law, far right. (Author's collection)

Mitchell's Terrace following the murder. (Author's collection)

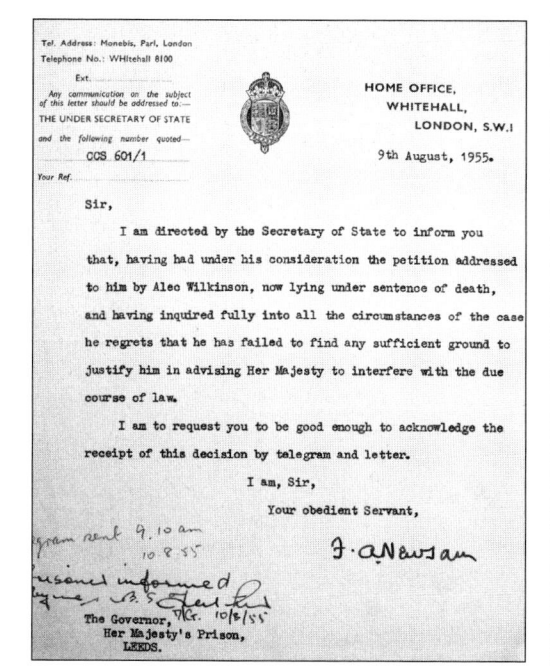

Letter confirming Wilkinson's execution will go ahead. (Author's collection)

Official notification posted on the prison gates. (Author's Collection)

A neighbour, hearing the cursing and sounds of a struggle, went to investigate, and as he entered through the front door and attempted to put out the blaze, Wilkinson let himself out through the back door and made his escape. He walked along the nearby streets and, on hearing the sirens of a fire engine, he approached a night watchman at a building site and claimed he had killed his mother-in-law. The police were called and as Wilkinson was taken to the police station he confessed to the crime.

Between fits of laughter he told an officer, 'I've done her in, the old cow... I piled the furniture round her... the wife walked in and I jumped her... if she gets over it she'll have a stiff neck for a week!'

Both women were rushed to hospital; for Clara Farrell it was too late – her throat had been cut, she had broken ribs and numerous stab wounds in her chest. Maureen was suffering from nothing worse than shock and bruises.

Tried before Lord Chief Justice Goddard at Sheffield Assizes on 22 June, Wilkinson pleaded extreme provocation and self-defence, claiming that Clara had wielded a bread knife at him before he stabbed her. He expressed no regret, and when asked whether he was sorry for what he had done; he said he was sorry for what he had done to Maureen. Asked if he was sorry about his mother-in-law, Wilkinson shook his head slowly and replied, 'No sir, I'm not.'

Following conviction, his counsel launched an appeal based on the biased summing by the trial judge, but it was rejected after a hearing lasting two days. A petition for his reprieve containing over 35,000 signatures failed to sway the Home Secretary and, as he was led to the gallows, Wilkinson turned to hangman Steve Wade and said, 'At least I know where I'm going, and can use a shovel!' It was a reference to his occupation as a miner.

It was the last execution carried out in Great Britain for almost two years, and the last carried out by Steve Wade. In 1957 the Homicide Act was passed which limited the crimes now liable to the death penalty. If Wilkinson had committed the murder in 1957 he would not have been hanged.

86

OVERWHELMING EVIDENCE

Ernest Raymond Jones, 10 February 1959

Thirty-eight-year-old Richard Turner was employed as a manager with the Co-operative society at the Cowms branch on Station Road, Lepton, Huddersfield. 'Dick', as friends knew him, was following in his father's footsteps in working for the 'Co-op', and having started as a counter assistant, he had risen up through the ranks to run his own branch.

Tuesday 30 September 1958 had been half-day closing in Lepton and that night, after supper, Turner drove the short distance to check on the building. There had been a number of break-ins at shops in the area and Turner wanted to make sure that all was well at the store. His wife became anxious when he failed to return home at the usual time and eventually she called at the store. His car was outside; there was a light on, but the door was locked and no one answer when she knocked.

Worried that something was amiss she called at the adjacent Liberal club and asked one of her husband's friends, Jack Howe, to accompany her back to the store. They then called for the assistant manager, Herbert Whittle, and the men entered the shop, returning moments later looking very shaken. Realising something was wrong, Mrs Turner hurried inside and saw the body of her husband

The Co-op store of Cowms. (Author's collection)

lying dead in a pool of blood outside the office. A post-mortem found that he had died as a result of a fractured skull and it appeared that he had been struck with a blunt instrument, which had broken the skull in five places.

The killer had left a distinctive heel print in the storeroom, made by an 'Avon Heel', a rubber heel that left a pattern of several small circles. It was a quite unusual heel, and boot makers in the area were questioned to see if they could offer any leads. It appeared that the killer had left a box near the counter filled with cigarettes and other easy to sell items such as hosiery and clothing. Missing from the safe was £76 in notes and change. It was reasoned that Turner must have disturbed an intruder in the store and that he had been bludgeoned to either prevent him escaping or maybe from identifying the thief.

Detectives began to interview anyone in the West Yorkshire area who had been convicted of any similar crimes, and two days after the murder they called at a house in Bradford and spoke to Ernest Raymond Jones. Jones was a 39-year-old Welshman who had been released from Armley Gaol earlier that year after serving a sentence for breaking into a store in Doncaster. He told detectives that he had been at home with his wife on that Tuesday night watching television. Satisfied with this account, police enquiries were concentrated elsewhere, but two days later police received information that questioned the truth of Jones's alibi.

Jones was told that witnesses had seen him in Huddersfield on the evening of the murder and he then changed his story and admitted that he had been in Huddersfield while his wife was shopping, but he was nowhere near Lepton. He was again released while enquires continued until finally, eight days after the murder, Jones was arrested and taken into custody.

A search of his house found the remnants of a pair of boots in a dustbin, which had been burned in a fire. These were taken to the North Eastern Forensic Laboratory at Harrogate, where they were found to have had an 'Avon Heel' which matched the imprint found at the Lepton store. Samples of paint found in Jones's jacket pocket also matched scrapings from the window, where the intruder had gained entry.

Jones stood trial before Mr Justice Hinchcliffe at Leeds Assizes on Monday 8 December, a courtroom to which he was no stranger. Opening for the prosecution, Geoffrey Veal QC, told the court that Jones was being charged with capital murder, that is murder in the course or furtherance of theft, and that there was 'well nigh overwhelming evidence to prove that Jones was the intruder who had killed the store-manager on 30 September.'

A witness was called who had spoken to Jones on the day prior to the murder, to whom he had claimed he was short of money and to whom he had offered to sell a large quantity of cigarettes. The landlady at the house where Jones lived with his wife testified that on the morning after the murder, she had seen Mrs Jones counting large amounts of silver coins, which she had then taken to be changed into notes. Jones had also told her to buy him some new boots, and he had then burned his old pair on the kitchen fire.

The most damning testimony came from Jones himself, who had told a police officer after his arrest that '... I was there. I just shoved him.' Jones maintained throughout that he had merely pushed Mr Turner when he was confronted with the manager at the top of the stairs and he had only done so to escape. He denied striking him with his fist, even though a witness told police she had overheard Jones telling his wife at the police station that he only given him a 'rabbit punch' to the head.

Defence counsel offered a plea of manslaughter, stating that at no time did Jones intend to injure the victim, and that although he had pushed Turner, this was only to make good his escape. Jones's counsel referred to the wording of the charge. Capital murder was deemed to

Ernest Jones. (Author's Collection)

be a 'murder committed in the furtherance of theft' and the defence made reference to the wording 'in the furtherance of theft', by claiming technically that the theft had been completed if Jones was ready to leave the store; the implication being that if the jury did find Jones guilty of murder, it would be non-capital murder warranting a prison sentence rather than the death sentence. After a three-day trial the jury found Jones guilty of capital murder. An appeal was launched on the basis that the murder hadn't been committed in the furtherance of theft, but the Lord Chief Justice dismissed the appeal, stating, 'if a burglar is interrupted and if he murders in order to get away it is still murder in the furtherance of theft.'

In the days of capital punishment in many prisons there were certain rituals involved when a condemned man is returned to await execution. At Armley a wooden chair was kept in the reception area, used exclusively by the condemned while awaiting transfer to their cells. It was part of the prison folklore that no one other than the condemned sat in the chair, and superstition had it that should someone other than a condemned prisoner use the chair then they would be fated to hang.

In the spring of 1958, a number of prisoners were helping prison staff clean the reception area. Unaware of the 'curse', one of the prisoners took the opportunity to rest his feet by sitting in the chair. He had been sitting for several minutes when a guard came in and shouted for him to get up, telling the prisoner the story behind this particular chair. The convict who had sat on the chair was Ernest Raymond Jones.

87

SINGLED OUT BY FATE

Bernard Hugh Walden, 14 August 1959

On Tuesday evening, 7 April 1959, 33-year-old Bernard Hugh Walden, a partially disabled lecturer in physics at Rotherham College of Technology, was midway through a lesson when a student reminded him he had promised to show them a past paper in preparation for their end of term exams. Walden told them he would go to fetch one and left the classroom. He never returned. Seconds later, shots rang out and two young people lay dead in the corridor.

Rotherham College of Technology at the time of the murder. (Author's collection)

Police officers were at the scene within minutes and learned that the dead were 20-year-old Joyce Moran, a typist at the college, and her 21-year-old boyfriend Neil Saxton, a student, also at the college, who lived with his parents in Sheffield. Although no one had seen the shooting, Walden, a member of a local gun club, became the immediate suspect when it was learned that he had abandoned his class and officers discovered he had a crush on the pretty typist. Piecing together what had happened, it seemed that Walden had happened upon the couple when he had left the classroom to collect the test paper. Seeing the couple laughing together, with Saxton leaning through the office window and Joyce sitting at her desk, had sent Walden into a jealous rage. He had then gone to his locker, pulled out his gun and committed a brutal double murder.

Walden had developed a crush on Joyce shortly after taking lodgings close to her home. He became friendly with Joyce's family and was a frequent visitor to their house, where, from time to time, he would watch television. He also took both Joyce and the family for trips out in his car, and would often give Joyce a lift into work before he moved to new lodgings across town. At some stage Walden had proposed marriage to Joyce, only for her to laugh off his proposal. Unbeknown to Walden, Joyce had been courting Neil Saxton for a few months and when he learned she had a boyfriend he felt it was his disability that had put Joyce off him. This had been compounded at a college dance when Joyce had danced with Saxton brazenly in front of Walden to the extent that he had told a colleague that if she ever made a fool of him again he would kill her.

The hunt for Bernard Walden lasted several weeks and involved officers across the country, along with Interpol. It ended in the early hours of 1 May, when Walden was spotted by a police officer as he slept in a park shelter at Reading, Berkshire.

Mr Justice Paull presided over Walden's trial for capital murder at Sheffield Assizes at the end of June 1959. He pleaded not guilty and offered a defence of diminished responsibility. His counsel outlined a catalogue of events that had culminated in the tragedy. Firstly, Walden had suffered the loss of his mother whilst at university, and finished with a disappointing third class degree. As a child he had contracted polio and this had left him with a withered leg, which made him bitter and deeply self-conscious.

'Walden believes he is a victim singled out by fate,' his counsel told the court. Described by his colleagues as a fine lecturer, Walden had become infatuated with the pretty typist and, through jealousy at the un-reciprocation of her feelings, he committed a brutal double murder.

The prosecution claimed there was no evidence of any signs of insanity nor any abnormality of the mind, and this was borne out by a statement Walden had made regarding the murders and how he regretted his actions.

Newscutting relating to the Rotherham murder. (Author's Collection)

'IF I HAD COUNTED 10 IT WOULD HAVE SAVED THIS'

After an absence of barely 15 minutes, a jury of 10 men and two women at Sheffield Assizes yesterday found Bernard Hugh Walden (33), former lecturer at Rotherham College of Technology, guilty of the capital murder of Joyce Moran and Neil Saxton. Walden's only trace of emotion as Mr. Justice Paull pronounced sentence of death, was to grip the dock-rail. His father, Mr. Reginald Vickers Walden, a 68-year-old printer, was not in court when the jury returned. Later he went to the cells to see his son.

It was disclosed that only a few days before the double shooting, Walden had received an appointment as senior lecturer at Barnsley Technical College.

CHIP ON SHOULDER

Dr. James L.M. Walker, senior medical officer at Leeds Prison, called yesterday by the Crown, said Walden had good reasoning powers and there was no sign of mental disorder. He had given a

Bernard Walden

Prison occurrence book detailing the last minutes in the life of Bernard Walden. (Author's collection)

'I feel dreadful about causing these deaths… if only I had the sense to count to ten it would have saved all this,' he told the medical officer at Armley.

On 1 July, the jury of ten men and two women took just fifteen minutes to find Walden guilty as charged and, white faced, he gripped the bars of the dock as sentence of death was passed on him.

88

A WIN ON THE POOLS

Zsiga Pankotai, 29 June 1961

Fortune had smiled on 50-year-old Eli Myers one Saturday evening in December 1960, when, along with fellow market traders and friends at the Jewish Jubilee Hall, Chapletown, Leeds, he was part of a syndicate the scooped over £15,000 on the football pools. Better known as Jack Marsh, bachelor Myers traded in men's clothing, and he was a well-known and popular figure at markets across West Yorkshire. For the last eighteen months Myers had lived in a house on Chelwood Avenue, Leeds, and during that time such was his preference for privacy the curtains had rarely been opened.

Once the cheque from the pools company arrived the money was divided out, and Myers became richer to the tune of £1,275. It was a handsome amount by 1960s standards and news of the syndicate's good fortune made the pages of the local newspapers.

On Friday night, 24 February 1961, Myers returned home from work to find an intruder inside the kitchen at the back of the house. What happened next was never clearly established, but it seems that Myers had interrupted a thief ransacking his house, presumably looking for the pools money. A struggle ensued and Myers received facial injuries and cuts to his hand, before he collapsed and died.

Eli Myers's house in Leeds. (TNA PRO)

Eli Myers' body lies between the French doors in the ransacked house. (TNA PRO)

```
GOVERNOR ORDER NO............
            Staff on duty              6.30 a.m.
            Instructors & T.A.         7.15 a.m.
            Breakfast                  7.30 a.m.
            Return from breakfast      8.30 a.m.
            Cease labour               4.10 p.m.
            Off duty                   4.50 p.m.

            EXECUTION OF - 3813 Z. PANKOTAI

1.  The execution of the above named prisoner will take place at 8 a.m. on
    Thursday, 29th June, 1961.

2.  Officer Waterhouse will stay with the executioners from the time of arrival
    at the prison until they have been dismissed from their duties.

3.  Breakfast will be served to the prisoner at 6.30 a.m.

4.  Prisoners reporting sick will be left in cells until 8.30 a.m.

5.  All trials left hand side A Wing to exercise at 7.30 a.m. on D.2.Wing.
    Remain until 8.30 a.m.

6.  Left hand side A Wing - convicted - to 1st classroom 7.30 a.m. Return
    8.30 a.m.

7.  Cooks party will return to kitchen from cells at 8.30 a.m.

8.  The main gate will be closed and will remain closed from 7.45 a.m. until
    8.15 a.m. except to admit persons necessary for the execution.

9.  Gate Officers
            Officer Wilson, D.         Officer Rawson.

10. The following will proceed to the execution shed at the appointed time:

            Chief Officer, P.O.W., Executioners, Sheriff, Governor,
            Senior Medical Officer, H.C.O. Hayes.

11. Officers Stephenson, Walsh and Newell will be on duty with the prisoner
    from 6.30 a.m.

12. P.O. Spooner will be responsible that the arrangements are rigidly adhered to.


                                              Governor,
                                              H.M. Prison,
                                              LEEDS.
```

Prison duties and details relating to the execution of Zsiga Pankotai. (Author's Collection)

Harry Allen carried out the last execution at Leeds. (Author's Collection)

When Eli Myers failed to show up on the local market stall the next day, his brother called at his house and found Eli lying on his back on the living room beside a French window, which had been broken. It was clear from the injuries Myers had sustained it was a case of murder, and as a pathologist carried out a post-mortem, detectives began to question neighbours. One neighbour told police that at 10 p.m. on the previous night she had heard sounds of a fierce quarrel, with bad language, raised voices and sounds of a violent argument that had ended suddenly. Asked why she had done nothing about it, the neighbour told the bemused policemen that this type of quarrel was an everyday occurrence in that part of the city and she had thought nothing more of it.

Detectives soon found a number of clues. Bundles of new clothing abandoned on wasteland near a lock-up garage on the outskirts of the city was traced to clothing stolen from Myers' van, which was missing from outside his home.

A more significant clue was found among some second-hand and bloodstained clothing discovered lying next to the bundled new clothing. This contained a jacket with a name written on the inside label, which in turn led detectives to a house on Woodland Lane, in the Chapeltown district, where, in the early hours of Sunday morning, they spoke to Zsiga Pankotai.

Pankotai, a 31-year-old Hungarian miner who lived not far from Myers, denied anything to do with the murder. There was, however, evidence linking the Hungarian to the murder: traces of blood belonging to the same group as Myers were found on the strap of his wristwatch, but most incriminating was a jacket found at Pankotai's house, one of a new batch Myers' had recently taken stock of. The jacket was identical to those in the van, and detectives reasoned that following the murder, Pankotai had simply swapped his own bloodstained jacket, found near the garage, for a new one taken from the van.

Pankotai appeared before Mr Justice Ashworth at Leeds Assizes on 24 April, charged with capital murder. Pankotai did not deny he had been in the house at the time Myers died, and thus his counsel put forward a defence of manslaughter. Medical witnesses were called to support his claim that while Pankotai had been responsible for the death of Eli Myers it was not a case of murder.

The defence claimed that Myers had died from natural causes and cited evidence from the pathologist that Myers hadn't died as a result of being stabbed or punched in the head. Professor C.J. Polson's post-mortem had found that Myers had received cuts to his hand, presumably caused when fending off someone carrying a knife, and that he had been punched hard in the face, which had resulted in a broken nose and displacement of his upper teeth. Death could have been caused by suffocation caused by blood from the nose and mouth filling the lungs, but Polson claimed that in his opinion Myers had died from shock, and that the victim was also suffering from heart disease.

Polson told the court that in his opinion, 'the injuries neither singly nor collectively were sufficient to have killed a healthy man, but in the presence of heart disease they caused his death.'

Pankotai claimed that he had only intended to scare Myers when, after being caught in the house, he had picked up a bread knife from the kitchen table. He claimed that Myers had lunged at him and in the ensuing struggle, which was alleged to have lasted almost thirty minutes, Myers died. Pankotai strenuously denied hitting Myers in the face with a chair, as the Crown had claimed, but he did admit that after the fight ended he had driven away in the victim's van, allegedly unaware if the victim was still alive.

After a trial lasting three days, Pankotai was convicted of capital murder and sentenced to death. An appeal was launched on the basis that the trial judge had unfairly rejected the evidence of Professor Polson but this was rejected, as was the leave to appeal to the House of Lords.

Hangman Harry Allen noted in his diary that the Hungarian weighed 148lb, stood 5ft 6in tall, and was given a drop of 7ft 6in. Zsiga Pankotai was the last man hanged at Leeds.

APPENDIX I

PUBLIC EXECUTIONS AT LEEDS ARMLEY GAOL 1864–1868

Date *Convict* *Executioner*

10 September 1864 Joseph Myers Thomas Askern
 James Sargisson

Newspaper account of the only public execution at Armley Gaol:

10th September 1864

The preparations at the prison for the execution were completed on Saturday morning and ample provision was made for the preservation of order among the crowd, which, even on the previous night, began to occupy the field in front of the gaol and the road which leads up to its gate. The scaffold had been erected during the day, but it was not until morning that its limbs were screened by the black cloth, which to some extent was also to hide the wretched men when they stood upon the drop, from the crowd beneath. The barricades on either side served in some measure to avert the gaze of the spectators, and were a safeguard against any eruption within the boundary wall which they might make.

As the hour of the execution approached, the spectators continued to pour in large numbers until the wide open space in front of the gaol and every available spot around were occupied. The roof of every house and mill, walls and even the lamp-posts were thronged with those anxious to witness the execution and there could not have been less than 80,000 to 100,000 people present.

There were also some hundreds of spectators on the Burley Road and near Woodhouse Moor, but they would be unable, except with the aid of glasses, to witness the execution. They were, speaking of the mass, of the class usually collected together on such occasions men employed in mills, factories, workshops, etc. with a not inconsiderable sprinkling drawn from a lower and more degraded Stratum of Society, but embracing a few of what were called 'the respectable class'. Here and there, until the fatal hour had nearly arrived, the thoughtless of the mass indulged in jests, and others even so far forgot the solemnity of the event as to engage in games of 'thimblerig' and 'fly the garter'. On the whole, however, their behaviour was quiet and orderly and many listened with evident attention to the scripture readers who, mounted upon stools, enforced the lessons which the occasion so impressively suggested. Amongst the crowd were a large number of women, many of them with children in their arms, and their anxiety, if possible, exceeded that of the men to obtain 'good views'.

APPENDIX I

Fears were entertained that the wound in the throat of Myers might open, and as far as possible to prevent such an occurrence Mr W.N. Price, 'Surgeon to the Gaol', applied plaster to the wound. About this time, both the prisoners appeared very exhausted, and before the pinioning Sargisson was so weak that stimulants had to be administered. Myers was exceedingly pale, but appeared to be more resigned to his fate.

At five minutes to nine, the bell of the gaol, which announced the arrival of the fatal hour, began to toll. There was then a cry from the dense multitude in front of "Hats Off", and almost immediately, the Under-Sheriff, Mr Keene, passed from the door to the scaffold, followed by the Chaplain in his canonical robes, repeating the funeral service.

Immediately behind him, supported on each side by warders, were the two prisoners, pale and anxious-looking. They knelt upon the drop whilst Mr Tuckwell most impressively continued to read the Service. Both of them uttered the responses and frequently ejaculated: "Lord have mercy upon me", and "Lord Save my soul". Mr Tuckwell, having pronounced the absolution, the executioner at once stepped forward, placed a white cap over the head of Sargisson and next over that of Myers. He then adjusted the rope upon Myers and after that upon Sargisson. Myers appeared quiet, but Sargisson shook his head and breathed heavily. Both of the men continued to call out "Lord. Save me!" and the last words uttered by Sargisson were to his brother murderer. He called out: "Ah lad, art thou happy lad?" to which Myers responded "Indeed I am!"

Instantly, with a solemn thud, amidst the hush of the multitude, the drop fell and the bodies were immediately completely hidden from the crowd. Myers seemed to die almost immediately, but the other man struggled violently for some minutes. The crowd, immediately after the drop, rapidly dispersed, though a number remained to witness the cutting down of the bodies at ten o'clock. A few minutes before that hour the upper portion of the screen was withdrawn – we suppose to allow the spectators then remaining to see that the sentence of the law was effectually carried out. It was then made evident how wise had been the precaution of concealing the bodies. Also that the fears entertained regarding the wound in Myers' throat were not without foundation. The results of the sudden drop had been to tear open the wound, producing in the throat an orifice sufficiently large to admit the insertion of a pocket-handkerchief and we are informed that blood flowed from the wound some minutes after the drop fall. In accordance with the sentence, the bodies were buried within the precincts of the gaol.

Sargisson, a 20-year-old labourer from Rotherham, and 44-year-old Myers from Sheffield, had both been found guilty of murder: Sargisson robbed and killed a man named John Cooper; Myers stabbed his wife to death and then tried to commit suicide by slitting his throat – surgeons prevented him from cheating the hangman.

Broadsheet recording the only public execution outside Armley Gaol, September 1864. (T.J. Leech Archive)

155

APPENDIX II

PRIVATE EXECUTIONS AT LEEDS ARMLEY GAOL 1875–1961

Date	Convict	Executioner	Assistant(s)
21 December 1875	William Smedley	Thomas Askern	
3 April 1877	John Henry Johnson	Thomas Askern	
25 February 1879	Charles Frederick Peace	William Marwood	
23 May 1881	James Hall	William Marwood	
23 May 1882	Osmond Otto Brand	William Marwood	
26 August 1884	Joseph Laycock	James Billington	
22 August 1887	Henry Hobson	James Billington	
22 May 1888	James William Richardson	James Billington	
1 January 1889	Charles Bulmer	James Billington	
31 December 1889 +	Frederick Brett Robert West	James Billington	
26 August 1890	James Harrison	James Billington	
18 August 1891	Walter Lewis Turner	James Billington	
5 January 1892	James Stockwell	James Billington	
14 June 1892	Henry Pickering	James Billington	
18 August 1892	Moses Cudworth	James Billington	Thomas Scott
4 April 1893	Edward Hemmings	James Billington	
3 April 1894	Phillip Garner	James Billington	
21 August 1894	Alfred Dews	James Billington	
31 December 1895	Patrick Morley	James Billington	
25 August 1896	Joseph Robert Ellis	James Billington	
17 August 1897 +	Joseph Robinson Walter Robinson	James Billington	Thomas Billington

APPENDIX II

Date	Executed	Executioner	Assistant
16 August 1900 +	Charles Benjamin Backhouse Thomas Mellor	James Billington	William Billington
28 August 1900	Charles Oliver Blewitt	James Billington	William Billington
29 December 1903	John Gallagher Emily Swann	John Billington	John Ellis
29 March 1904	James Henry Clarkson	William Billington	Henry Pierrepoint
16 August 1904	John Thomas Kay	John Billington	Henry Pierrepoint
20 December 1904	Edmund Hall	John Billington	Henry Pierrepoint
28 December 1904	Arthur Jeffries	John Billington	Henry Pierrepoint
15 August 1905	Thomas George Tattersall	John Billington	William Warbrick
28 December 1905	George Smith	Henry Pierrepoint	John Ellis
3 December 1908	John William Ellwood	Henry Pierrepoint	Thomas Pierrepoint
12 March 1909	Thomas Mead	Henry Pierrepoint	John Ellis
9 August 1910	John Roper Coulson	Thomas Pierrepoint	William Warbrick
29 December 1910	Henry Ison	Thomas Pierrepoint	William Willis
27 March 1917	John William Thompson	Thomas Pierrepoint	William Willis
18 April 1917	Robert Gadsby	Thomas Pierrepoint	Robert Baxter
17 December 1918	John William Walsh	Thomas Pierrepoint	William Willis
7 January 1919	Benjamin Hindle Benson	Thomas Pierrepoint	Robert Baxter
8 January 1919	Percy George Barrett George William Cardwell	Thomas Pierrepoint	Robert Baxter
6 January 1920	Louis Massey	Thomas Pierrepoint	William Willis
16 April 1920	Miles McHugh	Thomas Pierrepoint	Edward Taylor
6 May 1920	Thomas Wilson	Thomas Pierrepoint	Robert Baxter
30 December 1920	Edwin Sowerby	Thomas Pierrepoint	Edward Taylor
5 January 1923	Lee Doon	Thomas Pierrepoint	Thomas Phillips
28 December 1923	John Eastwood	John Ellis	Seth Mills
18 June 1924	William Horsley Wardell	Thomas Pierrepoint	William Willis
3 September 1925 +	Alfred Davis Bostock Wilfred Fowler	Thomas Pierrepoint	Robert Wilson Henry Pollard
4 September 1925	Laurence Fowler	Thomas Pierrepoint	Lionel Mann
7 January 1926	Lorraine Lax	Thomas Pierrepoint	William Willis
5 January 1927	William Cornelius Jones	Thomas Pierrepoint	Robert Baxter
2 September 1927	Arthur Harnett	Thomas Pierrepoint	Lionel Mann
7 January 1928	Samuel Case	Thomas Pierrepoint	Henry Pollard
14 August 1929	Arthur Leslie Raveney	Thomas Pierrepoint	Robert Wilson
4 February 1931	Frederick Gill	Thomas Pierrepoint	Robert Wilson

Date	Prisoner	Executioner	Assistant
28 April 1932 +	Thomas Riley John Henry Roberts	Thomas Pierrepoint	Robert Wilson Alfred Allen Thomas Phillips
6 February 1934	Ernest Brown	Thomas Pierrepoint	Robert Wilson
6 April 1934	Lewis Hamilton	Thomas Pierrepoint	Alfred Allen
1 January 1935	Frederick Rushworth	Thomas Pierrepoint	Stanley Cross
7 February 1935	David Maskill Blake	Thomas Pierrepoint	Alfred Allen
10 February 1937	Andrew Anderson Bagley	Thomas Pierrepoint	Robert Wilson
10 September 1943	Trevor Elvin	Thomas Pierrepoint	Harry Kirk
3 February 1944	Mervin Clare McEwen	Thomas Pierrepoint	Stephen Wade
31 January 1945	Arthur Thompson	Thomas Pierrepoint	Herbert Morris
7 September 1945	Thomas Eric Richardson	Thomas Pierrepoint	Herbert Morris
8 January 1946	William Batty	Thomas Pierrepoint	Harry B. Allen
30 January 1947	Albert Sabin	Stephen Wade	Harry Kirk
20 June 1947	Eric Charles Briggs	Stephen Wade	Harry Kirk
14 August 1947	William Smedley	Stephen Wade	Harry Kirk
21 August 1947	John Edward Gartside	Stephen Wade	Henry Critchell
7 January 1948	George Henry Whelpton	Stephen Wade	Harry Kirk
30 December 1948	Arthur George Osborne	Stephen Wade	Harry B. Allen
2 June 1949	Dennis Neville	Stephen Wade	Harry B. Allen
30 March 1950	Walter Sharpe	Stephen Wade	Herbert Allen
6 February 1952	Alfred Moore	Stephen Wade	Harry B. Allen
30 July 1953	Philip Henry	Albert Pierrepoint	Royston L. Rickard
5 January 1954	Robert William Moore	Stephen Wade	Harry Smith
27 January 1954	Wilhelm Lubina	Stephen Wade	Harry Smith
22 April 1954	Albert George Hall	Stephen Wade	Harry Smith
1 September 1954	Edward Reid	Stephen Wade	Harry Smith
4 May 1955	Winston Shaw	Stephen Wade	Harry Smith
12 August 1955	Alec Wilkinson	Stephen Wade	Robert L. Stewart & John R. Barker #
10 February 1959	Ernest Raymond Jones	Harry B. Allen	Harry Smith
14 August 1959	Bernard Hugh Walden	Harry B. Allen	Thomas Cunliffe*
29 June 1961	Zsiga Pankotai	Harry B. Allen	Harry F. Robinson

Barker present as trainee observer

* Cunliffe sacked for making an error at this execution

+ signifies double execution of prisoners not connected and hanged for separate crimes

INDEX

Allen, Harry 12, 111, 112, 126, 152, 153
Antcliffe, Henry 82
Ashworth, Mr Justice 153
Askern, Thomas 11, 18, 19
Avory, Mr Justice 66, 67, 78
Aziz, Shahad 16

Backhouse, Charles Benjamin 45
Backhouse, Frederick Lawder 45
Bagley, Ambrose 102
Bagley, Andrew Anderson 102
Bailache, Mr Justice 71
Baines, John 31
Baker, Alice 119
Baker, Percy 119
Ball, Charlotte 137
Ball, Det. Supt. John 139
Barker, Samuel 53
Barrett, Percy George 67
Batty, William 110
Beanland, PC 21
Beechcroft, Ada (daughter) 44
Beechcroft, Ada (mother) 44
Beechcroft, Annie 44
Beevers, David 35
Benson, Benjamin Hindle 66
Berridge, William 28
Berry, James 11
Beveridge, Det. Chief Insp. Peter 104
Billington, James 12, 26, 27, 30, 40
Billington, John 12, 49, 55
Billington, William 12
Binks, Lydia 98
Binns, Bartholomew 11
Blake, David Maskill 100

Blewitt, Charles Oliver 47
Blewitt, Mary Ann 47
Bostock, Alfred 78
Brand, Osmond Otto 24
Brett, Frederick 30
Brett, Margaret 30
Brett, Serg. 87
Briggs, Eric Charles 115
Briggs, Gertrude 115
Brisby, Dr Francis 98
Broadbent, Joseph 13, 15
Brooke, Mrs Margaret 35
Brown, Ernest 94
Bruce, Mr Justice 39, 48
Bulmer, Charles 29
Bulmer, Elizabeth 29
Burke, Dr William 29

Cardwell, George William 67
Case, Samuel 85
Castle, Elizabeth 91
Chamberlain, Frank 28
Channell, Mr Justice 52
Charles, Mr Justice 33, 36
Chatwin, Mr and Mrs Francis 52
Christie, John Reginald 13
Clarke, John 75
Clarkson, James Henry 50
Cock, PC Nicholas 21
Coleridge, Lord Chief Justice 58, 59, 60, 69
Collins, Mr Justice 40
Cooper, John 155
Cotterill, Mary 33
Coulson, Jane Ellen 59
Coulson, John Raper 59
Coulson, Thomas 59
Coulton, Jane 107
Cudworth, Eliza 37
Cudworth, Moses 12, 37

Dalby, John 52
Darling, Mr Justice 49, 53, 65

Darwell, Jane 72
Dennis, Kate 35
Dewar, David Walker 109
Dews, Alfred 40
Dews, Benjamin 40
Donoghue, Elizabeth 115
Donovan, Mr Justice 141
Doon, Lee 74
Doughty, Leonard 118
Duckworth, Bella 32
Dyson, Arthur 20
Dyson, Katherine 20

Eastwood, Ethel 75
Eastwood, John William 75
Ellis, Emma 42
Ellis, John 12, 13, 49
Ellis, Joseph Robert 42
Ellwood, John William 57
Elvin, Trevor 104

Fairweather, Mrs 141
Farrell, Clara 143
Finlay, Mr Justice 79
Finnemore, Mr Justice 128
Firth, Elizabeth 17
Fitton, Ellen 37
Foster, Evelyn 91
Fowler, Lawrence 80
Fowler, Wilfred 80
Fraser, Det. Insp. Duncan 132
Fraser, Mr Justice 82

Gadsby, Robert 63
Gallagher, John 48
Garner, Agnes 39
Garner, Philip 39
Gartside, John Edward 118
Gill, Alfred 92
Gill, Frederick 15, 89
Gilligan, Flora Jane 133
Goddard, Mr (Lord Chief) Justice 101, 102, 104, 145

Grantham, Mr Justice 34, 37, 41, 54
Green, Edna 124
Greer, Mr Justice 74
Grey, Nellie 110
Grey, Samuel 110

Habron, John 21
Habron, William 21
Hackett, Mary 139
Hainsworth, Emily 123
Hall, Albert George 139
Hall, Edmund 52
Hall, James 23
Hall, Mary Anne 23
Hall, Selina 23
Hallett, Mr Justice 110
Hamilton, Lewis 97
Hamilton, Maud 97
Hamilton, Mr Justice 61
Harnett, Arthur 84
Harrison, Hannah 32
Harrison, James 32
Hart, Irene 102
Hartle, William 86
Hawkins, Det. Serg. Dennis 139
Hawkins, Mr Justice 21
Hemmings, Anne 38
Hemmings, Edward 38
Henn-Collins, Mr Justice 115
Henry, Philip 133
Hinchcliffe, Mr Justice 147
Hindley, James 30
Hirst, Jane 51
Hobson, Eliza 27
Hobson, Henry 27
Holliday, Mary 29
Howe, Jack 146
Howell, Clara 58
Hoyle, Richard 39
Humphreys, Mr Justice 91, 96

Ison, Henry 60

INDEX

Jagger, PC Alfred 131
James, Emma 20
Jeffries, Arthur 53
Jelf, Mr Justice 55, 56
Jenkins, Mary 60
Johnson, John 11, 15, 18
Johnson, Julia Ann 63
Jones, Ernest Raymond 15, 147
Jones, Mr Justice 133
Jones, William Cornelius 83
Jones, Winifred 83
Joy, KC Commissioner H.H 98

Kay, John Thomas 51
Kay, Mr Justice 23
Kennedy, Mr Justice 42
Kew, PC John William 45

Lannen, Gordon 130
Laughton, George 133
Lawn, Gertrude 67
Lawrence, Mr Justice 50
Lawson, Insp. 17
Lax, Elizabeth 82
Lax, Lorraine 82
Laycock, Joseph 25
Laycock, Maria 25
Lee, Sing 74
Levine, Abraham Harry 129
Libman, Mr 118
Lindley, Mr Justice 17
Lopes, Mr Justice 18, 22
Lowe, William 23
Lubina, Wilhelm 137
Lumb, Albert 13
Lynas, Elizabeth Mary 50
Lynskey, Mr Justice 112

MacKinnon, Mr Justice 85, 87
Maloney, Sam 90
Manisty, Mr Justice 30, 31
Marwood, William 11, 12, 22, 23
Massey, Emily 69
Massey, Lewis 69
Massey, Margaret 69
Mathew, Mr Justice 26, 28
Mayne, Annie 66
Mayne, Charles 66
McCardie, Mr Justice 63, 64, 84
McEwen, Mervin Clare 105
McHugh, Miles 70

McLeod, Dr Neil 113
Mead, Clifford 133
Mead, Thomas 58
Mellor, Thomas 44
Moore, Alfred 15, 131
Moore, Isabella 84
Moore, Robert 84
Moore, Robert William 135
Moore, Ruth Elizabeth 65
Moran, Joyce 149
Morley, Elizabeth 41
Morley, Patrick 41
Morris, Mr Justice 121
Morton, Dorothy 94
Morton, Frederick Ellison 94
Mosley, Florence 27
Moss, PC Willis 33
Mottram, George 85
Mottram, Mary Alice 85
Myers, Eli 150
Myers, Joseph 154

Neild, Mary 20
Neville, Dennis 127

Osborne, Arthur George 123

Pankotai, Zsiga 150
Papper, William 24
Parkin, Alison 66
Parkin, Joyce 66
Parkin, Maurice 66
Parramore, Mildred 75
Paull, Mr Justice 149
Peace, Charles Frederick 20
Pearce, Mr Justice 143
Pearson, Mr Justice 132, 140
Pickering, Henry 36
Pickering, Jane 36
Pickering, Matilda 36
Pickering, Thomas 36
Pickford, Mr Justice 58
Pickles, Sarah 43
Pierrepoint, Albert 12, 134
Pierrepoint, Henry 12, 58, 60
Pierrepoint, Thomas 12, 58, 60
Plommer, William Francis 'Jock' 81
Pollard, Isaac 57
Pollock, Mr Justice Baron 29
Polson, Prof. C.J. 153
Porter, Mr Justice 100

Poskett, Marian 127
Prangnell, Serg. 87
Preston, Oliver 89
Pritchard, Mr Justice 116, 118, 120

Raveney, Arthur Leslie 87
Reaney, Elizabeth 76
Redshaw, Priscilla 44
Reid, Edward Lindsay 141
Richardon, Thomas Eric 109
Richardson, James William 28
Ridley, Mr Justice 45
Riley, Thomas 91
Roberts, John Henry 92
Robinson, Florence 43
Robinson, Joseph 43
Robinson, Walter 43
Roche, Mr Justice 71, 86
Rushworth, Frederick 98
Ryecroft, Frederick 24

Sabin, Albert 113
Sagar, PC 85
Sargisson, James 154
Saxton, Neil 94
Scott, Thomas Henry 12
Sewell, Amelia 18
Sharpe, Walter 15, 129
Shaw, Winston 142
Shelton, Harold 55
Sherratt, Elizabeth Maud 78
Siddall, Lily 74
Simmonite, Edith 117
Slade, Mr Justice 126
Slater, George 108
Slater, Mr Justice 73
Smedley, William (1875) 11
Smedley, William (1947) 117
Smith, George 55
Smith, Harry 13
Smith, Martha 55
Sowerby, Edwin 72
Stable, Mr Justice 105, 107, 136, 138
Stockwell, James 35
Stothard, Miss Ada 27
Streatfeild, Mr Justice 130
Swainston, Edith 70
Swann, Emily 48
Swann, William 48

Talbot, Joseph 101
Talbot, Mr Justice 76, 90

Tate, Jean Cave 142
Tattersall, Rebecca 54
Tattersall, Thomas 54
Thompson, Arthur 107
Thompson, John William 61
Thorpe, PC Frank 107
Tinsdale, John Henry 61
Tinsdale, Lily 61
Tucker, Mr Justice 104
Turner, Mark 105
Turner, Ann 33
Turner, Richard 146
Turner, Walter Lewis 15, 33
Twigdon, Thomas 31

Valentine, Dr James 140
Veal, Geoffrey QC 147

Wade, Stephen 12, 13, 114, 122, 137, 145
Waite, Amos 18
Wakefield, Violet 104
Walden, Bernard Hugh 148
Walker, Laura 109
Walker, Rhoda 67
Walsh, John William 64
Warbrick, William 60
Ward, Hannah 20
Ward, Lavinia 48
Wardell, William Horsley 76
Waterhouse, Barbara 33
Watson, Edward 135
West, Emma 31
West, Robert 31
Westcott, Ellen 76
Westwood, Ernest Hargreaves 123
Whelpton, George Henry 120
Whelpton, Irene 121
White, Arthur 141
White, Leslie 87
Whittle, Herbert 146
Wilkinson, Alec 15, 143
Wilkinson, Maureen nee Farrell 143
Wilkinson, Thomas 57
Williams, Mr Justice 25
Wilson, Annie 71
Wilson, Thomas Hargreaves 71
Wood, Serg. Sidney 108
Wood, Dennis 116
Woodcock, Edward 60
Wright, Mr Justice 35

Yeomans, Emily 10